THE JOSEPH FAMILY

EXTREME

EXCELLENCE

Publishing by

INSIGHT PUBLISHING

647 Wall Street • Sevierville, Tennessee • 37862

10 9 8 7 6 5 4 3 2

Disclaimer: This book is a compilation of ideas from numerous experts who have each contributed a chapter. As such, the views expressed in each chapter are of those who were interviewed and not necessarily of the interviewer or Insight Publishing.

Interior formatting and design: Brittany Stewart
Cover Graphic Design: Emmy Shubert

Printed in the United States of America

ISBN   978-1-60013-271-1

Contents

Message from Publisher

Excellence, as viewed by many people, is a standard very difficult to reach. Many people achieve success in some measure, but to reach extreme excellence is extraordinary.

We gathered several people whose life journeys embody the term "extreme excellence." In these interviews I asked what their thoughts were about excellence and what it actually meant to them. I also wanted to know why they believed the journey to excellence is a remarkable time in life. I received some very interesting answers—maintain focus and discipline, trust the right people, plan carefully, and more. Not only did I receive some very good answers but these successful businesspeople gave me several very practical step-by-step ideas about how to implement their ideas.

As one of our authors said, "The journey is simple but it's not easy; if it was easy then everybody would have a good one." The journey might be difficult but if we persevere, it is possible to achieve extreme excellence. Extreme excellence is a very worthy goal—in business as well as in one's personal life. No one should settle for less.

I challenge you to examine what these authors have to say and then try some of their suggestions. I am confident that if you follow their advice, you will be glad you did.

So set aside some quiet time, stretch out, and prepare for your own journey to extreme excellence!

David Wright, President
International Speakers Network
& Insight Publishing

Chapter 1

Karel Murray

David Wright (Wright)

Today we're talking with Karel Murray. Consistently ranked "outstanding" by organizations nationwide, Karel speaks, writes, and consults nationally on leadership, communication, management, and motivation. Karel owns and operates Our Branch, Inc., a national and international professional speaking and training company. She authored her first book, *Straight Talk—Getting Off The Curb*, with her sister, K. C. Lundberg, published articles in regional and national magazines, and offers a monthly on-line newsletter called "Think Forward!"®

Karel, welcome to *Extreme Excellence*.

What do you feel is the first thing a person must do to achieve excellence in his or her career and personal life?

Karel Murray (Murray)

As people, we understand that society influences us from an early age. Whether we are naughty or nice may very well depend upon whose point of view we are referencing. Our humor, sense of right and wrong, and basic personality are molded into an acceptable shape, fitting nicely with the cultural scheme of things.

Society is comprised of human prototypes of all sizes, shapes, and intelligence. As an efficient society, we love to place labels on personality types: poised, civic minded, snobbish, plastic, robust, rowdy, cute, ugly, creepy, dangerous, a lost cause. The list grows as we age, having established our own criteria for each category.

Consider meeting someone for the first time. You observe the person's face and actions—how he or she laughs, smiles, frowns, and reacts to you. Shift through your mental library—got it! Slap that label on and react according to personal programming. Labels help us orientate ourselves and determine the manner in which we interact with a specific type of personality. This keeps things safe and ensures our perspective is sound.

According to communications experts, when you meet someone for the first time, the first thirty seconds set the level of rapport. Call it chemistry. Unlike Captain Kirk who considers space as man's "final frontier," I believe these seconds are our greatest adventure. By utilizing labels to categorize people, we may fail to see what is not readily evident—a treasure trove just waiting for exploration. The greatest tragedy is the knowledge of others we might have learned yet threw away because we reacted to first impressions.

Standing hesitantly in front of thirty people in a karaoke session, an overweight woman stared down at her feet. I could hear the snickers of laughter and side comments about her appearance. Limp brown hair whispered across slumped shoulders as the stage lights glared off her sweating forehead. Her dress was shapeless and worn—completely unflattering to her generous figure. Still she waited patiently for the technician to begin her song. Jeering persisted from her well-dressed female friends as they urged her onward. Their faces registered the expectation that they would witness a delightful scene of embarrassment that they would gossip about at the office the next day. What was evident to me was that the singer's desire for companionship was so great that she would do anything to win their approval.

The music streamed from the loudspeakers with the opening musical accompaniment for "The Rose" by Bette Midler. And beauty entered the room. The lone singer's voice softly explored the corners of the room—emotional and true. A tremulous beginning transformed into an elegance and richness of sound; the room went mute. Incredulous looks were evident on many faces.

She sang to no one. She sang for herself.

As the music died away, the glow of exceptional talent dimmed. She stepped off the stage—once again the meek, subdued woman, oblivious to the surge of excited applause and chants for "More!" Shaking her head, watching the floor in front of her, she left the room.

I rediscovered that every person posses a niche in life—a purpose to fulfill, talents, and desires. The manner in which we discover these essential elements about others is entirely up to us.

Recognition of human dignity—cherishing differences—our final frontier.

What an adventure! People just need to engage!

Wright

Many people want to take the step (or engage), but doesn't life get in the way of achieving goals?

Murray

It is the weirdest feeling in the world—the lack of control. I've experienced it before when my son, Ben, was two years old and started a screaming tantrum in the toy department. He commanded attention from every passing mother, pleading his case for a new toy. His small grasping hands reaching out pitifully with wide open mouth howling his dismay—the scene was almost enough to do me in. What kind of a mother would deny her beautiful baby what his heart desires?

Obviously—me.

Now, I had options. I could have gathered him up kicking and screaming, tucked him under my arm, and marched out of the store. But, doing that would have denied me the pleasure of finishing a much needed shopping spree. So, I sat on the floor, placing myself at his eye level, and quietly waited for him to finish. He was a determined little beggar. For almost seven minutes he screeched his indignation—red faced, with tears streaking down his innocent cheeks.

Other parents looked at me quickly, shared a brief smile of support, and moved to another isle, hustling their children before them, hoping they wouldn't get the same idea as Ben's rebellion. Do you have any idea how long seven minutes is with a shrieking child? A lifetime. But, I sat resolutely, with a calm, patient look on my face, personally wishing for earplugs (putting my fingers in my ears didn't seem like the adult thing to do).

Finally, the tantrum dried up. He stuck his fingers in his mouth, sniffled, and came over to sit on my crossed legs. A heavy sigh leaked from his tired throat and he nestled into the crook of my arm. My gentle hug told him all was forgiven, but reinforced that Momma had control.

Yesterday, I felt that I was the one who lost control and desperately needed others to take over. Yet, I didn't know how to ask for it. Often, I've met up with obstacles and individuals who block my way to a dream, much like the tantrum Ben had years ago. I've learned now that I can't just sit down and wait for others to behave.

My control over situations is limited. All I can do is determine how I react to the roadblock and the options I create for myself, or give up control in order to move forward.

The wisdom comes in knowing which direction to take and we can be the only judge of that.

Wright

Sometimes the marketplace and economic reasons can impact careers, no matter how good you are. How do people keep things in perspective and move forward with their careers?

Murray

I actually had a friend by the name of David who came close to losing his job at fifty years of age. In the last corporate downsizing episode, David's family security was threatened—not just financially, but personal esteem plummeted. More disturbingly, he didn't understand why he was in jeopardy in the first place. While David prided himself on his diligent performance, attention to detail, faithfully relocating wherever he was needed in his twenty-year career, he believed his company valued his efforts—until the merger. He had to face the gut-wrenching realization that regardless of how well he performed, he was expendable.

So, rather than focusing on ways to self-destruct, here is some groundwork to plan for future career opportunities:

1. **Attitude.** Eliminate negative thoughts regarding your company's shortcomings. Instead, focus on becoming a lynchpin of positive energy and teamwork. Bring concerns or issues to management's attention succinctly and without condemnation. Provide solutions. Avoid placing your superiors in a defensive stance. I've learned that people tend to push back when cornered.
2. **Delay Gratification and Reduce Debt.** The significance of the debt accumulated by Americans is staggering. Debt eliminates options. It's close to impossible to feel any manner of security when financial liabilities outweigh income (living from paycheck to paycheck). Loss of income becomes less devastating when you minimize debt—you create room to react responsibly to unforeseen circumstances.

   Establish a workable financial plan now and begin by creating an emergency resource fund. Try to ignore purchases that are not essential until you have reached your goal.

3. **Education.** Use every opportunity to attend intriguing courses as well as those that provide specific job training for your current position. Consider concentrating on those topics that could develop into careers that would allow you to earn an income in an area you enjoy.

4. **Update Your Resume Annually.** Critically review your performance and achievements by writing them down formally in a resume. Outline your career objectives and evaluate whether your present situation fulfills those ideals. Early assessment of your evolution over the last year may determine a new career direction or alert you to an "at risk" current position.

5. **Network.** Get out and establish meaningful relationships with people in your industry or the field of your choice. In addition, set up informational interviews with businesses that interest you. Prepare for a planned career move either within your firm or to an outside company.

6. **Focus On The Target.** Chart the items that you consider important to you—your family, independence, career recognition, or net worth. If drawn in three or four different directions, this can be emotionally destructive and reflect in your performance and overall health. Clearly determine your top three priorities and plan accordingly.

Next time, when you want to react in a position of turmoil, ask yourself, "Can I afford the consequences?" This question is powerful in its simplicity. Work through your response in a manner that ensures that you stay on track with your true life plan.

Wright

What are some things people can do to create a state of mind that is focused on excellence and has a direct business impact?

Murray

I've discovered a growing phenomenon of professionals who seem to have "lost their way" in understanding their career paths. At one point, vision was clear and the path to success seemed to stretch on to a predictable future. Then, for no apparent reason, nothing feels or appears normal. This disruption in striving for excellence disrupts personal energy and creates undue stress.

A typical response to the stress may be the impulse to "change" everything—update the Web site, revise the logo, streamline services, add benefits, expand ad copy, buy better equipment, hire or fire staff—the list goes on. The sense of "losing the market" grips firmly onto the professional's perspective, which in turn creates an unfocused, sporadic, knee-jerk reaction to what might be a simple issue.

The level of self-imposed panic increases in direct relationship to the percentage of income earned from commission sales. The number of phone calls symbolizes the business barometer. When it flatlines—there's trouble on the horizon. Well . . . not necessarily.

Consider how a complex camera assembly works. Professional photographers understand the image needs to be isolated and brought efficiently into focus by the maneuvering of levers and dials. A non-professional usually purchases a camera that has "auto focus" where the camera is programmed to zero in on the image and, like magic, the camera adjusts and clarifies the field—simplicity at its best. That's because a set of instructions and logical processes are already programmed in the camera.

Autofocus is a concept you can apply to your business process by understanding that shifts in the market are bound to occur. Learn to adjust smoothly and effectively.

Evaluate Your Delivery Systems

Internal decline in processes often causes disruption in business. Are you delivering your product or service at the level of quality demanded by your market? Review your last ten to fifteen sales and evaluate the delivery system. Does it duplicate your "promise" to the public? If at first review it is at the level you want, consider calling the last five clients and conduct a short interview to see if the perceived disruption is non-system oriented.

For example: Your call prompts this client response, "Well, Mark, you always sounded so busy and rushed that I didn't want to bother you with little questions." Light bulb time. This could reveal to you how your tight schedule and elevated stress energy translates to the client as "you're too busy to bother" with their concerns.

A sad fact is that customers will gravitate to business professionals who only have eyes for them. They must be convinced of your total concentration and know you aren't thinking about the next deal, but are focused on them. Period.

If, however, the responses from your inquiries are positive and in line with your expectations, move on.

Gain Perspective

Speak openly and honestly with other business professionals in your field. It will not only expand your knowledge and expertise, it will open doors to future referrals. Consider establishing a mastermind mentoring group that consists of people in your industry who:

a) Are successful in what they do,
b) Have a competence and expertise in areas you need to develop,
c) Are ethical and trustworthy,
d) Will also benefit from the association of other group members.

Assemble a group of fewer than ten members and establish quarterly meetings designed to address industry issues, personal development, and feedback on projects. I'd encourage a broad cross-section of participants from different parts of the country—remember, it's about perspective and expanding the focus field.

If this isn't practical, then read—a lot! Dedicate thirty minutes a day to personal development. This practice could dramatically impact your overall ability to anticipate future trends and probable growth or decline issues to address for your business.

Research Outside Influences

Have economic changes created a tidal wave of panic? Access the Internet and analyze what others are doing to address the issues you are concerned about. Are your sales declining due to lack of consumer confidence in your industry?

Don't hesitate to establish a dialog with your past customers and clients. Understanding their perspective may be more valuable than you know.

Look Inside

Careers are not necessarily easily matched to emotional temperament. If your first reaction is despair and excess worry to a last-minute crisis, change, or business slump, you probably won't last long in your position. If you mentally can't handle the assault of extreme ups and downs and the consequences of your career results in the destruction of your health, perhaps a reevaluation is necessary. Career choice does matter.

Analyze the Need

The public and client rules. If your service or product is deemed a "luxury item" in a down-turning economy, your business may be the first to be negatively affected. Create a list of benefit statements that will re-establish need as defined by the current environment. Determine how the services or products you offer can become a "must have" in the marketplace. Remember, it's all in how you present it in relation to the current public concern.

Update Your Business Plan

Revisit the goals, objectives, and input you have gained as a result of your investigation and update your business plan accordingly. Establish a budget that accommodates changes and remember to build in flexibility. When you are prepared financially to cover the natural "slumps" in production, you will be less likely to negatively overreact. Following a well-built, consistent plan enhances the sense of personal control and minimizes the impact of a slowing marketplace.

In this day and age of rapidly shifting attitudes, loyalties, and expectations, you need to establish your business identity as "solid ground"—like the lighthouse beam that guides ships to safe harbor in foggy conditions. World changes may speed by for the public, but you and your business should always remain in their line of sight. Stop flailing around in a self-imposed fog. Set up your equipment, take aim, and click.

Wright

If these steps you have described are taken, is there an essential element that also must be in place in order to ensure business professionals actually achieve the results they want?

Murray

They have to make a decision. It's not as if people are making a choice between life and death when business planning; they only have to determine how their business will grow over the next two to five years. All we have to do in order to achieve our goals is to commit. No excuses, no lop-sided rationalizations—just set one foot in front of the other and take the first step. Whether that first step will falter or stride confidently forward is determined by attitude and strength of belief in our own skills, attributes, and character.

Guillermo del Toro, Hollywood director, carries this phrase with him wherever he goes: *"In our choices, lies our fate."* And this is exactly what scares the daylights out of me. All of us have our priorities. No one else sets them for us—we do. We either say "yes!" to a choice or we set it aside. My fear is that I'll say "yes" for all the right reasons, yet find out later that my decision set in motion another entirely separate chain of events.

Our fate and future depend upon how well we know ourselves. My husband, Rick's, decision to drink a glass of red wine occasionally for health of his heart nudges me to take equally good care of myself. The yoga CD is unwrapped and ready for viewing. I just need to put it in the computer and discover introspection, meditation, and physical health. "Make-a-decision" time has arrived and it is time to set the plan in place. And I realize it is a relatively simple process.

COMMIT

C – Calibrate: Now is the time to adjust schedules and projects so that a balance of business and personal time exists.

O – Observe: By making an effort to truly understand the finer aspects of your business so that you can avoid professional pitfalls such as overbuilding, under-staffing, growing too fast, or absorbing a debt load that is unmanageable.

M – Manipulate: As the details are drawn up, the business model and tasks defined, each element that falls into place creates the momentum to surge forward with focus and wide open eyes. Business professionals need to move the pieces around until they feel they have a sound path to follow.

M – Memorize: Spending a few moments every morning to review specific goals and objectives will ensure that your personal engine is finely tuned and ready for high level performance. Your unconscious thoughts will automatically help you make decisions that are tied directly to your life goals.

I – Implement: Your plan of action steps are viable and well thought out. Initiating the business-building processes you have designed will give you purpose and reinforcement emotionally. You know you will be able to move forward in your career, much like placing your foot on the gas and shifting into gear.

T – Trust: Sometimes "disobedience is the preamble to responsibility," according to del Toro. You have developed a thoughtfully laid out plan, spent resources to research options, and envisioned a future that belongs to only you. Learn not to waste a passing glance at those who will try to make you conform to their vision. This dream is yours alone. You have to trust your instincts to allow yourself to succeed.

Living your life with gusto, purpose, and focus should be your goal— grasping the future with both hands in enthusiasm, no matter what it brings. Live your life like Buzz Lightyear and yell, "To infinity and beyond!"

Wright

Karel, you often talk about excellence in terms of personal courage. What do you think courage is about and how does it actually impact excellence?

Murray

Stopping a runaway train and saving all on board—that's courage.

Stepping in front of a bus to push a small child out of the way—that's courage.

Facing the world with a blemish on your face—that's courage.

Wearing a safety pin in your pants, praying it won't pop open at the worst time—that's courage

When I was growing up, my primary resource for understanding the concept of courage was the Wizard of Oz on television—watching the odd foursome face peril after peril. Confront the Wicked Witch of the West? No way. The Cowardly Lion had it right—clanking knees, shaking shoulders, a quivery voice, and cowering in a corner. Hopefully that evil person wouldn't see him.

But then he did a strange thing. Despite his overwhelming fear, he still did the right thing. He faced the Wizard, spoke up to the Witch, and battled flying monkeys. Why did he do that? If he just faced the other way, walked in a different direction, or bowed his head appropriately, he could have gone on with his life as the overlooked, insignificant being he wished to be. Instead, he stuck his neck out.

So why did they call him the Cowardly Lion when in fact he never was? He just experienced those typical human emotions that set us on a path that is ours to choose.

So what exactly defines courage? "The very word comes from the heart—*coeur* is the French word for heart. It comes from the gut. Follow your heart—another way to make a brave decision" (excerpt from *What is Courage?*—Michael Useem, *Fast Company* magazine, September 2004).

"A strong emotional commitment. When you run up against barriers that keep you from those ideals, the stronger your commitment, the more likely you are to take action consistent with those ideals. We are where we've been." —John Kotter, Professor, Harvard Business School.

My hero—a quivering mass of fur dancing along a yellow brick road. I've discovered through the course of my life that I've learned five very important lessons from the Cowardly Lion. Perhaps sharing these with you today will help you face this ever-changing, fast-paced, sometimes overwhelming world:

1. **You can beat up a flying monkey.** Often in our lives we are annoyed by the buzzing and interference of subtle criticism shielded as kind consideration. For example, a friend says, "You look lovely today! Maybe if you lost a couple of pounds, that outfit would drape better." This is accompanied by a squeeze on the hand or a pat on the cheek. The buzz begins to get so loud, you can't even view yourself in the mirror anymore without considering what others will say about the outfit or your "not twenty anymore" figure.

   The incessant drone drowning out a positive self-image. Unwelcome thoughts darting around the brain, much like flying monkeys swooping around the Lion.

   Distraction, attack, restrain—a technique mastered by the flying monkeys. However, this can be effectively countered by using candor—your willingness to speak the truth. I've learned that when someone pays me a compliment and then slaps me in the face with a well-intentioned criticism, I ask him or her to repeat *only* the compliment. I let the person know (in a kind way) that I'm aware he or she has my best interests at heart, but comments regarding the weight I'm already highly conscious of takes the joy out of the initial compliment.

   Some of you are flinching right now thinking, "I can't possibly say that to a friend!" Personally, I believe that if the friendship is true and sound, honest communication between individuals not only strengthens the relationship, but you can enjoy the partnership with delight, not fear the dreaded well-meaning comment.

2. **The person behind the Big Wizard head is human.** As a child, I stood in awe of celebrities, managers, and public officials—the stern policeman addressing my sixth grade class on the values of not using drugs, a doctor probing my throat and announcing I had to have my tonsils removed, or the mayor of the town waving from an automobile during a festive parade. Their glamour, authority, and absolute control made them icons in my childlike perspective.

   Some of us never lose this automatic fear of authority. For example, let's say you receive a letter with an attorney's name and address on the envelope. The first reaction may be "what did I do?" Your hands might actually sweat as you slice open the envelope. Then a burst of laughter erupts when you realize it is only a solicitation for a local charity event. Your thundering heart slows and you can actually hear again because the blood that rushed to your ears has receded.

This adrenaline rush, shortness of breath, blushing cheeks, and copious sweating are all signs of facing up to The Big Wizard Head! The Cowardly Lion experienced all of these symptoms, yet he still stepped forward to present his request. Granted, he was pushed forward and then he ran down the hallway after being yelled at, but heck, we all have our moments.

As I've aged, I've learned that I can have this affect on others without even knowing it. I'm a mother, I served as a Regional Manager, I will be President of a national association, and have served as a community Chamber of Commerce Chairperson. Others treat me respectfully, and some actually experience anxiety when they speak with me.

But—it's just me!

Once the mantle of authority is placed on our shoulders, the assumption of power over others' lives settles in. It not only takes courage to stand firm in front of an authority figure, but our own outward display of courage is absolutely critical. Lacking this element of leadership will unsettle those around you. However, you can't be something you are not. People will know that you are faking it and then your credibility plummets.

If you are a Big Wizard Head, wear a great hat, a smile, and interact with confidence. If you have to face a Big Wizard Head, communicate with style—wear a better hat and a broad grin. It may look like a snarl if your lips are clenched too tight in fear, so loosen it up, enjoy the moment, and address any issue that might come up with confidence and purpose.

3. **You can melt your own Wicked Witch.** The broom-riding, intensely green, beady-eyed Wicked Witch of the West completely terrified me. It wasn't just her hawk-like appearance and focused efforts to destroy the Lion and his companions; it was her complete control over the flying monkeys and Munchkin Land inhabitants.

That is what parents can feel like. Now, I wouldn't be here if it wasn't for my parents, but, really, when are we allowed to grow up? As I think of my son, Ben, I flash back to when he was two years old and needing a hug after a fall from his Hot Wheels. But now he is twenty-eight years old, six foot three inches tall, and ready to take on the world. How come I still feel that my sage advice is critical to his essential wellbeing? Why do I analyze every decision he makes and feel compelled to offer unsolicited guidance? Oh no—I've become the hawk mother equivalent of the Wicked Witch!

Focus on the childling. Regurgitate substance for life enhancement. Shove him out of the nest, but fly underneath him, ready to catch him if he falters in his flight.

My husband learned how to melt my Wicked Witch tendencies. It's called restraint. A quick kick under the table, a hand squeezed urgently in my lap, or "Karel, let's get dessert," to cut off the conversation. I receive these signals and I melt, right on the spot. I recognize that he is preventing me from stepping over the boundaries and forcing me to allow our son to grow up.

But it's so darn hard! That is where courage comes in.

"If you do the thing you think you cannot do, you'll feel your resistance, your hope, your dignity, and your courage grow stronger. You will someday face harder choices that very well might require more courage. And when those moments come and you choose well, your courage will be recognized by those who matter most to you. When your children see you choose, without hesitation, without remark, to value virtue more than security, to love more than you fear, they will learn what courage looks like and what love serves and they will dread its absence"—*Faith of My Fathers: A Family Memoir, Worth the Fighting For,* and *Why Courage Matters,* U.S. Senator John McCain and Mark Salter.

Melt your own Wicked Witch with love. Dorothy did it, so can you.

4. **No forest can overwhelm you unless you let it.** According to Michael Marshall's *The Upright Man* we each feel that we are unique, but then we discover that—along with many others—we accumulate property, pay debts, fulfill obligations, and then watch while our replacements take on the role in society that we can no longer retain due to advancing age. It's a life cycle that keeps repeating itself, generation after generation.

Creeping through the dark forest on the way to stop the Wicked Witch, the Cowardly Lion and companions are attacked by aggressive, groping trees. Fighting back gallantly, they manage to disengage themselves and continue on with their mission. Our lives can be like those trees. Consider the television programming designed to reach out and make you "addicted" to watching night after night. Don't read, play board games, sew, or other creative endeavors, just relax and let us entertain you. It is enticing and unrelenting.

Limiting our view on the world is relatively easy. Just put blinders on, read news from only one source, and keep focused on your daily duties and responsibilities. This is the right thing to do in society! But don't you want more? Getting involved with others and the community is a way to elude the grasp of the trees. It doesn't involve money, just heart and courage. Establish your own direction because you can.

"Courage is a function of feeling part of a social fabric, of a network that's going to do something that has never been done before. When Caesar spoke, people marched. Getting people to march behind your ideas takes courage."—*Warren Bennis.*

5. **The Lollypop kids are really frightening—run—run fast!** Strange, unexpected things occur in our lives all the time. Dorothy, accosted by those dancing, singing triplets called the Lollypop Kids, appeared frozen in place while their perfect shrill harmony pierced the air. You know how it happens—life is moving along smoothly, and then *bam!* In prances a situation you least expected.

You aren't sure whether you should laugh, cry, or get angry. Sure, we've perfected the art of "ventilating" to our closest friends: "You wouldn't *believe* what happened to me today!" But our ability to control our lives is slipping away more every day. It's addressing these times in our lives that requires strength of character, action plans, and support systems.

To this day, the Cowardly Lion remains an icon for me. He reminds me that our own acts of courage create the texture of our existence.

- Rosa Parks refused to sit at the back of the bus, altering race relations nationally.
- Christopher Reeve inspired the world trapped within the confines of a wheelchair.
- Nelson Mandela confronted an African nation about abuses and inequities.
- Norma Rae blew the whistle.
- A teenage girl births a child and gives it up for adoption.
- Parents send their children off to school for the first time.
- A three-hundred-pound woman has a gastric by-pass and loses one hundred and fifty pounds.
- My father learns to dance so he can share a moment with his daughter at her wedding.

- One hundred and twenty-five days without an alcoholic drink and the woman smiles.
- A man and woman say "I Do!" and mean "Until death do us part."
- A twenty-nine year old young man endures chemotherapy— determined to live a quality life.
- Dying, a person in hospice says, "That's enough," and says goodbye to those he (or she) loves.
- A hug of forgiveness.

Courage is the capacity to wait until you've learned as much as you can and then take action. You have to take gambles and learn more.

"There is no such thing as a safe risk. . . . All courage is risk!"—Warren *Bennis.*

Wright

Excellence, as viewed by the masses, almost seems to be unreachable. As we conclude this interview, what are your thoughts about what excellence actually comprises and why you feel the journey to excellence is a remarkable time in our lives.

Murray

Have you ever been startled into sitting up when you've read an article? That happened to me while reading "In Praise of the Purple Cow" by Seth Godin printed in the January 2006 *Fast Company* magazine. I almost spit out my coffee in uncontained excitement as comprehension finally crashed over me as I read, "Today, the one sure way to fail is to be boring! Your one chance for success is to be remarkable."

To be remarkable—to be excellent—that's the brass ring we leap for as it swings just beyond our grasp. That's where the problem lies. How do we know when we're being remarkable?

A whole slew of questions rebounded in my mind: What if we are too self-absorbed or busy to recognize brilliance in a simple process-altering idea? What if our brains constantly generate new revelations but it seems like everyday common stuff to us? How do we know we haven't had a remarkable idea, and then blew it off because we were bored by it?

What if being remarkable is a state of mind we already live in but fear of failure keeps us pinned down? I don't know about you, but I don't want to be boring! I want to live, jump out of the moving train, stretch out to clasp the brass ring, and cling for as long as it takes to make the goal—swinging in the wind of change and totally exposed.

You and I both understand that when we take chances, public opinion can go two ways: Part of the crowd will think we are idiots, pure and simple. They won't hold back, letting us know how stupid we are to give up a great job with a solid income to pursue a dream that is so filled with competition that we are bound to fail. The head-shaking dismay is enough to make us run for cover. However, it's the other fraction that fills the sails for the journey. Their eyes light up, genuine smiles of pure promise drive straight into your heart. And we can breathe again. They will never think we are boring or unsuccessful. We had the guts to try.

I've watched *American Idol*. The focus of the program shows us how many purely awful singers and wannabes there are out in the world. And they are held up for our ridicule and laughter. Granted, it was sobering to see the number of individuals who never should have auditioned. But audition they did. That is what kept me watching—over 100,000 people vying for the one *American Idol* spot, and they still tried. Now that's remarkable.

So, who says you won't have the one "out-of-the-box" idea that will carve a new direction for business?

Step up to Excellence

1. Structure your idea around your area of brilliance. Believe in the possibilities.

2. Make sure you have the passion and ability to move your idea forward.

3. Have a vision of what your idea will look like. Keep your description simple as you identify how your idea will transform the market.

4. Plan carefully and do your research. Learn who, what, where, and when!

5. Trust the right people. Negotiate relationships with professional resources (attorney, accountant, and marketing guru).

6. Gain a thorough understanding of the legal knowledge regarding your idea.

7. Seek funding by considering a variety of sources.

8. Maintain discipline in doing your documentation and tracking profitability.

In order to step up to excellence, become totally focused—like a dog with a steak bone. Once a dog gets a good grip on the bone, it will shake off all outside influences that try to take it away. Dogs are tenacious about maintaining a tight hold on the prize.

Get a grip. Be excellent. Be remarkable.

About the Author

Karel Murray, a national motivational humorist and business trainer, is the author of *Straight Talk: Getting Off the Curb,* a book co-authored with K. C. Lundberg, *Think Forward!*®, a monthly e-newsletter with more than 4,500 subscribers, *The Profitability Blueprint Series: Career Building Concepts for the Real Estate Licensee*, and numerous articles in local, regional, and national publications.

Karel Murray
Our Branch, Inc.
2731 Ragley Drive
Waterloo, Iowa 50701
866.817,2986
karel@karel.com
http://www.karel.com

Chapter 2

Ricky Dawson

David Wright (Wright)

Today we're talking with Ricky Dawson. Ricky thought for years about the statement of whatever the goal was as being only a fraction of the whole. An example is football—"this game is 10 percent blocking and tackling and 90 percent attitude." Since he played football for a long time, someone should have at least mentioned something about the 90 percent part. The answer is you can't teach what you don't know. Looking back on thirty years of business experience, Ricky says he can say without a doubt that attitude is a huge part, maybe not 90 percent, but at least about 50 percent. The attitude part is much more important when things are not going as planned. It's easy to be positive and motivated, Ricky says, when the road is downhill and the wind is blowing from behind, but let that change just a bit and you need someone who can coach the two faces of attitude, outlook, and insight. In an interview a couple of years ago, Michael Jordan made a statement similar to this when asked if he thought of himself as the greatest basketball player of all time. He said, "You could argue who was the best forever, but never forget I always needed a coach." Ricky thinks the same is true about attitude—you really need a coach. If you need a coach for skills, you need one for attitude. Harvey Mackay, the famous author and speaker, has eighteen personal coaches for everything from training to humor.

Ricky, welcome to *Extreme Excellence*.

Ricky Dawson (Dawson)

Thank you David, I appreciate it. You and I have been looking forward to this day for about twenty years.

Wright

Ricky, how do you spell success?

Dawson

I spell it A-T-T-I-T-U-D-E. I think, when looking back on all the stuff that's happened in my life, attitude was probably the most important part and probably the hardest to understand. From "you'd better change" your attitude to "you have to have the right attitude." All that sounds great but where and how do you get a new one and will it be a good one? There are a lot of attitudes out there you don't want!

Wright

How do you measure attitude?

Dawson

You can measure attitude a lot of different ways. We measure attitude by the amount of things that we have acquired and by the distance one has run. But one thing I'm totally convinced about is if you somehow manage to get to the top of the heap and you are all by yourself, the journey wasn't worth it. I think success is your self-worth divided by the amount of life you have managed to live. It is also measured by how many crap storms you have weathered and if you are pushing forward.

I've had one partner in my life who thought that things would bring him happiness and he's probably the most miserable person I've ever been around; but he has a lot of things.

You've got to be able to look back and love that person in the mirror. Find the things you have a passion for and do those things. You might find your passion for things on the outside after you're paid your dues for a living, but if you can manage to incorporate your passion as your living, you will never have to do the four letter word—*work*. Of course, you've got to be able to pay your bills; it's hard to have a great attitude if you can't pay attention, but you have to balance the scale. When you do the balance thing, put your thumb on the passion side of the scale and tilt it toward the passion side.

Wright

You and I have been friends for years and you've told me consistently down through the years that if you can't sell the product—or just as important, if you can't sell people on your dream—you can't reach your goals. Is that still true?

Dawson

Selling is just part of the deal—it's ongoing. We are being sold all day every day by television, radio, billboards, newspaper ads, and the list goes on the on and on. Selling has gotten a bad name because sometimes the salesperson calls at the wrong time or won't take no for an answer. Remember, salespeople are trying to make money and you are trying to keep yours. The secret of this game is to get on the other side—find something that other people not only want, but have to have and build the bridge to that something and own the bridge. Then you can enjoy the game of selling.

For salespeople who are pests, I ask them for their home number so I can call them when they are busy at home and try to sell them my products. Most of the time they just hang up.

Wright

I have seen you build several businesses. In one business I saw you toil for years and years with all kinds of problems and things that you had to overcome. What do you think is the hardest thing to overcome when building a business from the ground up?

Dawson

I hardest problem is getting everyone on the same page. Everyone in the group may not have the passion for the project that you have so you have to continue to sell the deal over and over almost daily. It's the same at home—your spouse may not have the same passion for your widget as you do, but you have to keep selling her or him over and over. Having a little success from time to time helps sell the deal. A lot of people believe just the things they see. To reach great goals and experience life in its fullest you have to be able to see things as they should be or could be and not as they are.

In fact, I just found a diamond in the rough. In Genesis 11:6, God comes down from heaven and people are building a tower to reach Him. God says, "As long as they are one people and all speak the same language, nothing they imagine will be impossible." That pretty much sums it up. If we as a company, state, or even nation will all pull together, we win. But it's only possible if you start with a passion for the goal because the critics are just waiting to steal your dream.

Wright

Will you describe attitude for our listeners and for our readers?

Dawson

Attitude is strange; it's like trying to hug a cloud. Every time I think about attitude it reminds me of what Bear Bryant said about class. The legendary coach of Alabama said, "I can't exactly describe what class is but I know it when I see it." Attitude goes further and deeper. I can't probably explain it in one sentence or less, but I can tell you that I know a good attitude when I see it. I can pick a good one in a crowd (of course, you can pick out the bad ones also).

When we start thinking about attitude and its importance, we wonder what it is and why we have the attitudes we have. When I was building these companies from the ground up, which is where I like to start because it gives us a good foundation, I came to the conclusion that attitude is a combination of two things. We've always thought about it as our outlook—trying to stay positive, like the glass is half full or half empty (mine is the one that runs over, but you can have either of the other two). In reality, it's that plus how we look and think about ourselves. Even more important than this is we can't let other people's attitudes affect us. Every relationship you'll ever have in your life is either going to be positive or negative. Don't get me wrong, there are some relationships that will be neither, but I don't have a lot of those. Pick out the people you most would like to be like and associate with them. In real life you do this without thinking about it. The five closest people in our lives affect us in ways we could never realize. They help us up or bring us down.

It was so funny, coaches tried to sell us the idea that this attitude thing had something to do with football when in reality, the three sides of football are the game, the coach, and the player. Of these three only two can have an attitude. Of course, attitude affects the game but it is all between the coach and the player. The game has no attitude, you bring it with you.

Wright

So it's a combination of outlook and insight—in other words it's a two-way street.

Dawson

Yes, it's a two-way street—you can't just keep on giving it away, you have to receive it from somewhere. I remember this as a kid playing ball. There was a time when I didn't want to take the last shot. I didn't want the ball to be hit to me. I didn't want to bat when the bases were loaded and there were two outs in the ninth; I wanted someone else to do that. Then all of a sudden, one day I start realizing that's this is what it's all about—it's about taking the opportunity. There's an old statement in basketball: you miss 100 percent of the shots you don't take.

I read something about Michael Jordan regarding how many times he took the last shot and didn't make it (and there were many in his career). But you don't think about his missing that last shot, you think about his taking and making the last shot. See, it was his attitude that allowed him to miss a couple and still take the chance.

Wright

So if you say that you receive attitude, where does it come from?

Dawson

You have to find the places where you can get fed. It's really not any different than your body. To have a healthy body we can't just eat junk food all the time. Even more important than the things that go into our stomach are the things that go into our minds and our hearts. I think that those are just as important as the things that we're eating—good things in, good things out. I have even come to the point where I think that often it's not what we're eating that's killing us, but it's what's eating us.

I knew there was more to this attitude stuff, but I was from rural Louisiana; not a lot of time is spent in long discussions about attitude. One morning walking to class, a classmate asked me if I had ever read or listened to any of Napoleon Hill materials and I said I didn't know who he was. He walked back to his room and gave me Hill's book, *Success Through a Positive Mental Attitude*. I read a couple of pages and found a new world. The next couple of days I cut class and stayed in the library.

Of course that's all we do now—we meet people who have ideas and visions and become involved with them. Thirty-five years later, I'm going to be honest with you, I don't need a lot of positive reinforcement. I don't need a bunch of cheerleaders on the sidelines keeping me in the game. But you know what? I enjoy it. I think that's what I enjoy about the speaking business more than anything. It's not the boastful thing of getting in front of a crowd and being able to do it because very few people can. The real reason I enjoy it is after a session when someone comes up to and says, "I didn't really want to come to this but I am so happy because what you said was what I needed today!" Knowing that what I am doing is helping someone makes the difference.

My first experiences on the outside with positive driven people, were multiple groups—a small number of churches. These were charismatic churches and they were pretty small back in the '70s. They were just getting their start in our area; but if you "fed at their trough" you had to be a part of their group. That was a turnoff for some people. I just thought there was a better way to do it. I thought there was a way to carry the message of attitude and teach it without having to sell product. Actually, you are the product. This process is about selling you on you.

After my playing career, a lot of things happened and I really did not care much for the game. It had paid for my education and in my mind and heart the games were over. A group of local kids needed a coach and one of the dads came out here one afternoon and he and I sat out and talked. I said, "Well, I'm going to tell you something Merlin, I'm not the guy you're looking for,"

"Why is that, Ricky?" he asked. "You're the only guy in town who's played a little college ball."

"Yeah," I replied, "but I don't care anything about the game. Some things have happened through the years. I don't know if the trip was worth it or not."

"Do you think you can do it better than they did?" he asked.

I said, "Yeah, I know I could do it better."

"Well, here's your opportunity right here."

So I went up there and that year we won a state championship. We had a lot of fun and built relationships that have lasted a lifetime. The trip was worth it because it taught me the attitude part and the journey to find the one you desire.

Wright

I remember that you told me some time ago that the problem for most people is figuring out that a part of your being is missing. You were talking about a friend of yours, Bill, who used to say we're all a little crippled. Is that right?

Dawson

Yeah, Bill's saying was cute and true—we are all a little crippled. We all have problems; we all have heartaches and disappointment. It's part of the game. Bill was an alcoholic and I hate to admit it, but he was never a recovering alcoholic. He said the right things, he pushed the right buttons, and "played the right music," but within a couple of days, weeks, or months his wife would call a say, "Bill is late from work." That meant Bill was drinking and when that happened he drank for a couple of days. You see, I'm always late but I don't have any excuses. The whole thing was an excuse for Bill to return to his self-pity and have a party. And then after a couple of days he'd return to us to feel sorry for him. And then one day is wife quit playing his game and Bill went away. I loved Bill but I could not help him with hurting myself.

Wright

Do you think, Ricky, that attitude can be taught?

Dawson

I know it can be taught, but to start with, it has to have been caught. For example, when I was coaching football, one or two guys would catch my attitude, and then it took a few days—maybe a week or two—and then it was like a wildfire, it burned slow for a little bit then all of a sudden everybody's on fire and most of them didn't know how or why. Then I would reinforce it with stories, poems, and games. I just kept it going. At that point they knew they wanted it and actually, at that point, they didn't need me anymore. I want to be their coach, but if I don't teach it to them, they'll find it.

Wright

So let's say I had a need to get a better attitude and of course you're a coach, so now what?

Dawson

Well, what we're going to do is we're going start a process. This reminds me of a story of two little boys who were born into a family. One the sons was always positive, he was always happy with everything no matter what was going on. The other one was always negative. At Christmastime the dad was talking about it one day and he said, "I'm going to do a little test here." In one room he put every toy that he could think of that the kid who had a negative attitude might even think he wanted. Then for the kid who was always positive, he brought him a big old pile of horse manure and dumped it in the middle of the room.

The next morning he went in and the negative kid was sitting in the middle of the floor. The dad walked in asked him, "What's the matter?"

With tears in his eyes the boy said, "Well, I wanted a blue train and I wanted a bigger ball and I wanted a train that went around in circles—" He wanted this and that and everything was either the wrong size, wrong color, or totally wrong.

The dad walked into the other room and there's manure everywhere. The kid with the positive attitude was running back and forth just digging through it."

"What in the world are doing?" the dad said in surprise.

The kid said, "Man, Daddy, with all this horse manure in here there's got to be a pony somewhere!"

What we have to do is exactly that, we have to dig through the mess that has been piled on us over the years—all the negative things that have happened in our lives.

When I was coaching with other coaches through that period of time I was amazed when I would sit down and we'd talk about drills. I'd say this is what we are going to do, what about you?

One of the coaches would always come up with one of these drills, like a bull in the ring or a play that had not been outlawed yet.

I would ask, "Well, why do you want to do that? There's not even a place in the game where that exists. When you put people around in a circle and you let somebody run as fast as he can from behind and knock you down I would say that that's a penalty—it's clipping—why would we teach that in practice?"

Of course the response would always be, "Well that's what we did; that's what they did to us."

My response was, "Was it fun?"

Of course the answer was always, "No."

"Well, why would you do it then?" I would ask. "Why would you punish them because you were punished?"

"Oh. Okay—makes sense."

We have to learn from things that we didn't like or that wasn't fun, or wasn't right. An example is that living in the South, certain prejudices were things we had to overcome. We lived in them and we saw people who had them, but most people my age didn't want it anymore. They just dropped it and went on with their lives. The phrase that I always use is: the journey is simple but it's not easy; if it was easy then everybody would have a good one.

Wright

How long do you expect this journey to last?

Dawson

Well, David, mine is going to last my whole life or whatever part of life I have left. I'm "over the hill" now—I'm past fifty-five. I remember when I was a kid one time asking my daddy how old he was and he told me he was fifty-five. I thought to myself, "Whew! That's old." I think about that every time I turn another year older. But I think that not only will it last the rest of my life—whatever part I can say my life is—but it's also going to last after that. If I have a positive affect on the people I meet, my family, my grandkids, the people I'm in business with, heck, David, long after I'm gone, they'll see something or hear something or have an experience that reminds them of me—something I said or did—and they might just smile or they might even laugh out loud and guess what, I'll be there, if only in their thoughts.

Of course in a negative way, it could be the same thing. Just think about the possibility of having negative experiences with people all your life even after you're gone. The same thing will happen to them—something negative will remind them of you, and they'll think of you. So either way, we live on. I'd just as soon people have positive memories of me.

Wright

One way we teach is by example. I have known you now for two decades and I know your wife. I know you to be a good father and I know you to be a good husband. Two of your kids I've seen grow up, and both are "chips off the old block," either that or "chunks off the old hunk," as my son says. One of your kids is a college football coach, the other one coached a while in college.

What is the connection between coaching a parenting?

Dawson

Until I was a parent, I did not understand the connection. One of the most important things is to live what you preach. Don't be confusing. Be very careful about what you say. When they mess up, never, ever say, "I figured you would do that." They carry what you say, but they believe what you do.

Wright

Ricky, I really appreciate all this time you've taken with me today to discuss this really important subject. I'm really glad that you're in the *Extreme Excellence* book. This is going to make a great chapter. I think people are going to get a lot out of it.

Dawson

Appreciate it David. I've known you for years and I wanted to tell you this. I spoke a good bit about ten years ago and I looked at the mark and saw what I wanted to do. I made a conscious decision to get this business started so I could vault my career off this business. I had had some struggles in my life and I had thought about it a lot. I knew what I wanted to do fifteen years ago when we first met, but because of my circumstances and my inability to actually make a living the way I wanted to back then, I didn't act on it. I made a conscious decision to do that and I really thought this project would take four or five years. During the holidays this year— between Thanksgiving and Christmas—it's been fourteen years. I guess the point of this is it doesn't really matter whether it has taken four or five or fourteen years, the thing that matters is that I get the job done and have enough time left over to pursue the dreams that I've always had.

I think our biggest problem in this country is we come in from work in the afternoons and we watch three or four television shows that have a beginning and an end, which makes us think our dreams should come true in an hour two, but it's not always that way. You have to work and protect your dream until the day you can actually live it. That's just the way it is.

Wright

Today we've been talking with Ricky Dawson. Ricky is called "The Attitude Coach" and you don't have to guess why, based on what he's said here today. I think that he's brought some great insights into the world of attitude. He's a great father, he's a great son, he's a great husband, and to me he's a great friend.

Ricky, thank you so much for being with us today on *Extreme Excellence.*

Dawson

I appreciate it David. I'm looking forward to seeing you at the next workshop.

About the Author

Ricky thought for years about the statement of whatever the goal was as being only a fraction of the whole. Let's say football: the statement "this game is 10 percent blocking and tacking and 90 percent attitude." Since I played it a long time someone should at least mention something about the 90 percent part. The answer is you can't teach what you don't know. Looking back on thirty years of business experience I can say without a doubt that attitude is a huge part, maybe not 90 percent but least around 50 percent. The attitude part is much more important when things are not going as planned. It's easy to be positive and motivated when the road is downhill and the wind is blowing from behind, but let that change just a bit and you need someone that can coach the two faces of attitude, outlook and inlook.

Ricky Dawson
The Attitude Coach
1732 Allen Lane
Clinton, LA 70722
225-683-9292 Office
225-413-8543 Cell
attitudecoach@gmail.com
www.theattitudecoach.com

Ricky Dawson

Chapter 3

Garry Parker

THE INTERVIEW

David Wright (Wright)

Today we're talking with Garry Parker. Garry has a bachelor's degree in Criminal Justice from Concordia University and is a licensed law enforcement trainer in Texas. His ability to educate through entertainment makes him a delightful instructor. Garry uses a little southern humor to entertain and connect with his audience. He has dedicated more than twenty-five years to serving the people of the State of Texas as a police officer. After serving in enforcement for over twenty years, Garry moved to the position of Public Information Education Resource Officer. Once in the education field Garry began developing entertaining and educational presentations on topics such as traffic safety, personal safety, security, and leadership. He has won five state awards and three national awards for Excellence in Program Development and Presentation. Garry has served as a keynote speaker for many local, state, national, and international conferences. He has appeared on national television and radio and in the national print media. Garry is considered to be a leader in the prevention of school violence, workplace violence, and domestic violence. He is a traffic safety consultant and has developed a driver safety training course for use by drivers of all ages in an effort to reduce crashes, injury, and death.

Garry, welcome to *Extreme Excellence.*

Garry Parker (Parker)

Thank you, David.

Wright

So after serving in law enforcement for over twenty years, what prompted you to move into the education field?

Parker

After many years serving as a Texas State Police Officer, I had witnessed so much death and destruction that it was really starting to take a toll on me. I had gotten to the point where I didn't like myself, didn't like anybody else, and I needed a change. It was a tough time but I knew I needed to do something different.

I started praying for God to give me a new outlet, whatever that would be. My prayer was, "If You give me a different job, I'll do everything I can to honor Your name and to do what I can to pass on your word." Well, you need to be careful when you make promises like that to God because He may not have the exact same idea for the outcome as you do.

A position in safety education opened and I was selected to fill the position. Shortly after I went into the field of education, two boys walked into Columbine High School. That single tragedy changed my focus and what I thought the job of a safety educator would entail. I began developing programs around school safety, and I got heavily involved in school violence and prevention. It was a new and different challenge and I took to the job like a duck takes to water.

Wright

You talk about bringing focus to the job; will you tell our readers a little bit about that and how it applies to law enforcement agencies?

Parker

In law enforcement, over the last few years, we have had more death to police officers caused by motor vehicle car crashes than being shot and killed feloniously. In January of 2006 I was part of the detail that was going to bury a young police officer killed in a car wreck. When I am on a detail to play taps at the funeral of a Police Officer I make it a point to never look at the body—it's just a self-defense mechanism.

After we had folded the flag back the funeral director came in and opened the lid of the casket. I stood there looking at this young man. Every bone in his body had been broken; he didn't look anything like the pictures I had seen of him. It was at that point when I really started getting a passion for finding ways to stop police officers from being killed by motor vehicles.

Shortly thereafter, the Texas Department of Public Safety lost three more of its troopers and all three of those were killed in one-vehicle car crashes. I took the deaths of those young men personally because it seemed that no one else would. I developed a program titled, "Bringing Focus to the Job." As police officers, we often feel as though we're invincible—we're nine feet tall and bulletproof. That attitude runs rampant across our profession, and "Bringing Focus to the Job" takes a look at why these guys are dying, how they are dying, and what we can do to prevent it. My goal with the program is to take it to every police agency in this country. It is my mission during the last part of my career, and the last part of my life, to end senseless death to police officers due to car crashes.

The job of a police officer is dangerous enough as it is; what I would like to see happen is to never have to go to another funeral for a police officer who was killed because of a car wreck.

Wright

In your national award-winning presentation, "If a Car Could Talk," you give five reasons people are killed in traffic crashes. Will you tell us what they are?

Parker

The five main reasons that people die in car crashes are: speed, failure to wear your seatbelt, driver inattention, driver fatigue, and driving under the influence. Most crashes involve two and three of those factors.

Speed: In Texas we have so many wide open spaces that speed has always been a problem. When the federal government set the speed limit at fifty-five back in 1973 (the Fuel Conservation Act of 1973), not only did Texans not like it, but Texas police officers didn't like it either. Part of the reason was because of the way the law was written. Texas police officers were enforcing seventy miles per hour in the daytime, and sixty-five at night. Because of one stroke of a pen and the way the law was written, it was no longer safe to drive at the speed limit that had been set the day before. Texas police officers took a negative view of that and we did not enforce the speed law as we should have.

It wasn't long before people realized that we were being lax about the speed limit and they became lax in watching their speed. Now here it is 2008 and we have the same problem, however, instead of the speed limit being fifty-five miles an hour, the speed limit is seventy; people are driving eighty and eighty-five miles an hour. The cars that we drive today are not designed to withstand car crashes at those speeds.

Seatbelts: There is one undisputable truth to wearing seatbelts and it was proved reliable by Sir Isaac Newton when he said an object in motion remains in motion until acted upon by an equal or greater opposing source. There are so many police officers who will say, "I've never unbuckled a dead man." Well I have—I've taken their heads out of windshields, and taken steering wheels out of their chests, all with their seatbelts intact. The fact is, vehicles today are not designed to withstand the crash forces of the speeds we drive. Wearing your seatbelt increases your chance of surviving a crash by 60 percent. To me, that's better than the alternative. Many agencies across the country have taken a zero tolerance policy. What that means is we no longer issue warnings for seatbelt violations. The purpose for the policy is a life-saving mission; it is not a revenue-gathering scam. It seems that if we can't educate people to the right reason to wear a seatbelt to gain voluntary compliance, then we have to get in their wallets.

Driver Inattention: For some reason it seems that people believe that driving requires very little skill. If you look at the requirements for obtaining a driver's license anywhere in the country, you'll see that the requirements are very minimal. Because of those minimal requirements the average person believes that driving is easy, and because they believe driving is easy, they will use driving time as a downtime. You can see anything you want to see in traffic anymore. I've seen women putting on makeup, men shaving, and people brushing their teeth. The very best (or worst, depending on how you look at it) that I ever saw was a lady putting on her pantyhose driving down the road.

When I stopped her I asked her, "What are you doing?"

"I'm putting on my pantyhose," she replied.

I thought, "Man, you know, how late do you have to be to be driving down the road putting on pantyhose?" As I walked off I thought, "If I had stopped her twenty minutes ago, what would she have been wearing? Would she have come out of the house in a towel and gotten dressed?"

I'll tell you what, David, the more that I work in traffic, and the more that I'm around people, the more I realize that this is not a joke. If somebody told me that he or she saw three naked men riding a pink elephant the only thing I'd ask them is which way they were going. Nothing shocks me anymore.

Driver Fatigue: This is a huge problem, and not just in traffic. Fatigue is a huge problem in society because people don't understand human beings need to sleep. The average human body requires eight hours of sleep to be able to operate properly. Now, we can condition ourselves down to about six hours, but if you start getting less than six hours on a regular basis, what you do is build what's known as a sleep deficit. Sleep deficit is a problem because you have no control over when your body shuts down. There have been times when I've had to work twenty-four-hour, thirty-six-hour, and forty-hour disasters where I may not be able to go to sleep for up to forty straight hours. At about hour twenty you get real tired, and about twenty-four you get a second wind that lasts only for about an hour and a half or two hours. Then you start saying things that don't make sense because basically you're just walking around sleeping with your eyes open—that's about all you're doing.

There are people who will deprive themselves of sleep for reasons that I can't understand. Maybe they want to stay up and watch television or they've got this or that to do. I understand that there are issues with sleep, but there is only one cure for fatigue and that is sleep. Maybe you're lucky enough to be sitting behind a computer terminal typing away after lunch, and you fall asleep; when you wake up there are three pages of z's. But most of the time people are driving down the road, in traffic, and their minds are wandering. Then they start slapping the back of their neck trying to stay awake. The problem with fatigue, however, is that people deny the fact they've got a problem. They think, "I can make it—it's just another five miles, or another ten miles—" There are times when people will take micro naps and wake up in the middle of a ditch or wake up against a telephone poll or not wake up at all.

Driving Under the Influence: This has been a passion of mine since I went to work in education. To me, America has a tolerance for innocent deaths in their own country where they won't tolerate innocent deaths in someone else's. If you think back to when America started bombing Baghdad, General Tommy Franks was the Commander of the Overseas Forces. He gave daily news briefings, and he was being hammered about the number of innocent civilians being killed. He tried to reinforce the fact that the use of smart bombs, and striking strategic locations would keep the innocent deaths down to a minimum. But in America, drunk drivers will kill sixteen thousand people a year on average and nobody cares as much. That just blows my mind. Many people look at alcohol as our "golden calf" because society is run by the golden rule right? He who has the gold makes the rule, and the industry has lots of gold. Until society gets really serious about the fact that alcohol is killing people, we're always going to have a problem.

I heard the story of a family that lost their twin daughters. The girls were seventeen years old. They were coming from a job at the mall. A nineteen-year-old in a pickup ran a red light and killed both of them. The young man went to court and was found guilty of intoxication manslaughter by the jury. The defendant went to the judge for punishment, because usually judges are a little more lenient than juries are. The judge found him guilty and charged him. The defendant was sentenced to five years in the Department of Corrections but the Judge would probate that sentence for eight years because the he hated seeing anyone that age ruin his life over one little mistake. David, you know, I would hate to think of what I would do if I was in a courtroom and someone referred to the death of my little girl as "one little mistake."

To cure society's ills, America is going to have to take the stance that there is no "safe" level of alcohol when it comes to operating a motor vehicle. America will also have to start holding those who choose to consume alcohol and drive accountable by revoking driver license privileges, seizing vehicles, and selling them at auction, then handing down harsh penalties for drunk driving. Drivers who cause deaths when they consume alcohol and drive should be prosecuted for murder rather than intoxication manslaughter. The cure is almost too simple for government work! If you know you will be consuming alcohol, you don't get in a vehicle and attempt to drive yourself home.

You know, society is going to have to get serious about these five primary causes of vehicle crashes or we're going to continue having Americans perish at the hands of mechanized death.

Wright

With the number of automobile accidents daily in our country, do you feel that society has become hardened to death?

Parker

I think society uses traffic crashes as a way to decrease the excess population—you know, thinning out the herd. If we had a plane crash (plane crashes are news media events) with 150 people killed aboard an airliner, the entire country gets up in arms. But that many people are killed on a daily basis in car crashes and people either don't notice it or choose to ignore the facts. Car crashes are a huge problem in society and until we start viewing their occurrence as an epidemic and start training to improving our driving skills and our attitude toward driving, then people will continue to die.

Trying to push for annual or semi-annual training on safe driving will always be an uphill battle because of the attitude of society.

Wright

So what safety measures can our readers take to reduce the chances of being injured or even killed in a traffic crash?

Parker

Know the rules. If you don't know the rules, take it upon yourself to learn the rules. Once you have learned the rules, follow those rules. Drive the speed limit, wear your seatbelt, get plenty of rest, don't drink and drive, make sure you pay attention to the task of safe vehicle operation, and give the other fellow a break. You know, really, all we have to do is just to be a little friendlier as a society behind the wheel and we wouldn't have near the number of problems that we have.

Wright

As an advocate of safety in the workplace, you say that prevention is everyone's responsibility. So what can an individual employee do to prevent workplace violence?

Parker

The U.S. Postal Service identified workplace violence as a major concern between the mid-1980s to the mid-1990s. The massacre at the Edmond Post Office (Oklahoma) in August 20, 1986, that resulted in fourteen deaths and seven others wounded gave society the term "going postal," which meant a person was on the edge going on a killing spree. The gunman died of a self-inflicted gunshot wound to his head. The gunman was postal worker Patrick Sherrill who was known to his co-workers as "Crazy Pat." His behavior had been odd for quite a while. Now, I don't know about you, but to me, if people in my workplace are referring to an individual as "Crazy Pat," I think that as a supervisor I would want to know why and get to the bottom of it.

What we're trying to teach employees and supervisors in Texas is that we can't know all of our employees personally, but if we see people we do know having problems, let's try and get them some help. As individuals we have to know our co-workers. Supervisors need to know their employees, and if they will make it a priority, maybe not push the issue when someone is just having a bad day. Just try and find out a little more about what's going on in the employee's life other than what is happening at work.

We encourage employees to wear security badges so that people will know when someone is where he or she is not supposed to be. We also try and teach employees to challenge those who do not look as if they belong. I'm not talking about walking up and saying, "Hey, what are you doing here?" I'm talking about walking up and saying, "You look like you're lost. Can I help you find something?" That may be all it takes to get an individual who is there for mischief or criminal intent to leave. I believe these few things would help us to reduce the workplace violence issue.

Wright

In your statistics on domestic violence, you state that domestic violence victims lose eight million days of paid work annually. You also state that 68 percent (which sounds really high) of company executives agree that domestic violence training would benefit their companies financially. You say that 56 percent of supervisors are personally aware of employees who are victims of domestic violence daily. Given these facts, why in the world are companies not holding training programs to reduce the problem?

Parker

My opinion is that domestic violence is society's ugly little secret. Everyone's mother told us not to talk about what happens inside the family to people outside of the house. I believe that even though that was 1950s and 1960s mentality, we're still bringing that attitude to work with us when it comes to domestic violence.

Domestic violence is an ugly situation. It is a dangerous situation and it is an embarrassing situation for the people involved, and they don't want to talk about it. Companies that would spend a little bit of money on domestic violence training may end up having to get involved in the employee assistance program as well.

One service we provide to our employees is an employee assistance officer. Our employee assistance officer stays very busy. When she is notified of an employee who is having issues with domestic violence she quickly goes into action. (if the employee wants help,)then our Employee Assistance Officer will do everything in her power to get assistance to that employee no matter what the need is—financial, emotional, etc.

Eight million working days a year are missed by people who are dealing with domestic violence. Can you imagine what kind of productivity we'd have in this country if we could just cut that in half? Sixty-eight percent of company executives say, "Well, our company could probably benefit if we were to train on this subject, but then again, you can lead a horse to water, but you can't make him drink." And even though your company provides training in domestic violence, getting employees to attend the training is a different story.

Then 56 percent of supervisors are personally aware of employees who are victims of domestic violence daily. They see the bruises, they hear the phone calls that upset the employee, and they see that fatigued employee and they just don't do anything. I don't think they really want to get involved that deeply in someone's personal life. It's the same old thing that society has said for years: "I just really don't want to get involved." There are times when people need to get involved because some of these people can't help themselves. They're afraid of what's going to happen to them—they're afraid to step out of the situation because staying in a bad situation beats the fear of the unknown. Eventually someone is physically harmed to the point where the company's insurance has to pick up some of the tab for the injuries; this can get expensive for the company.

Wright

You have a presentation titled, "The Games Children Play." Will you tell our readers how to educate parents, teachers, and communities about the influences children face daily that induce school violence?

Parker

If we were to look at the big school violence events, Columbine, Virginia Tech, Paducah, we can see the lessons we have learned from some of these children who have killed their teachers and fellow students. (I call them "children" because that's what they are). I believe that there are influences they face daily from the media that parents do not understand. Some children are affected, some aren't; but as parents and teachers we really need to get a grip on what these children are doing. I've have studied video games described as a "first-person shooter." As the player you are actually the shooter. I think some of these children learn shooting tactics from these video games, and they get to the point where they are hardened to the reality of death.

I've told the story many times about a very dark time in my life when I was lonely and I felt like nobody cared about me. I was just really going through some serious problems. I had seen so much death and destruction in my life that it was really starting to take a toll on me; I seriously considered taking my own life. Right then I realized that all I needed was just to go to sleep. When I woke up things weren't better, but I did feel better about myself, so I went and sought help.

What I learned was the average person is born with the ability to deal with a certain amount of death and destruction. You're supposed to eventually go through the loss of your parents and your grandparents. Perhaps you'll lose a couple of friends, but if you ever get beyond the area of the normal loss of family and friends, as I had, your reaction becomes abnormal. I had gotten so hardened to death that I could sit and eat a sandwich while they were doing an autopsy. And what I learned through my therapy process was that people are only given a limited ability to deal with these situations.

The reason I tell people that story is not for the readers to feel sorry for me or for them to call me and set up a group hug where we can sing "Kum By Ya." I tell the story because our children are playing video games and they're watching people die; even though it's electronic—it's a game—they're still seeing people die.

I've got a video clip I use in this program. In that one-minute-thirty-second video clip you witness twenty-eight murders, including the killing of three police officers. Now, I know that has to be taking a toll on some children. Now again, I'm not saying that everyone who plays these video games will have these issues, but I think that the children lose sight of reality. I wonder if any of those children who went on killing sprees in their schools thought, "All I've got to do is put a quarter back in this machine and these people will come back."

I just think as a society—as teachers and parents—we really need to get a grip on what our children are doing. The same thing with music (and my god, I hope I don't sound like my dad), but if you listen to the lyrics in music that constantly degrade women to where they're not much more than an object, you wonder. How long does it take to develop the mindset that behavior portrayed in music, video games, and movies is normal behavior?

You can see the influences of those things in the way our children speak in public. I have been in the Marines, I have been a police officer for years and years, and profanity is part of that society. I have done everything I can to reduce the amount of profanity that I use because I had a college professor who said that profanity makes your ignorance audible. When you're not smart enough to say something else, you use profanity.

I've thought about how profanity came into society. I guess that in the beginning it was used to draw attention to something. Now, in today's society, profanity no longer has a shock factor. As a matter of fact, if you don't use profanity, you probably shock more people than if you do.

Wright

So do you feel that affective leadership in the workplace, school, and at home can increase safety measures?

Parker

Oh I believe so, and I'm not just talking about parents and teachers, I'm talking about building a core of students. There are students who are born leaders, but I think that if schools would get together and find ten or twelve underclassmen and start developing those students as leaders, when they become seniors they could take over the leadership role of the school.

Can you imagine what a school could do with a peer group of ten or twelve leaders who have been trained, who could then mentor their peers, and use reverse peer pressure to change the way a school works? That's what I'm all about—I want to see tomorrow better than today. Then I want to see next year better than last year, and better than it was when I first came here.

I believe that by training a group of leaders in a school or a workplace or in the home is just absolutely imperative for our society in order to increase safety.

David, my little girl is nine, and she will be going to high school soon. I'm running out of time to make a difference for her but just maybe together we can make a difference in the lives of others.

Wright

So what advice can you give our readers to help them ensure safety at work, at home, and on the roads?

Parker

We should take personal responsibility for our own actions. Be totally focused on what you're doing. We can't allow ourselves to have our attention spread out in so many different directions. Whether you are on the job, shopping, on the road, or at school, you need to constantly be reminded that your personal safety is important.

We need to be watching everything. We in police work use the term "Code White" as a code for the awareness level (you just woke up, you don't know where you are or what's going on) that's a very dangerous mindset to be in when you are in public. We also use the term "Code Yellow" as an awareness level (cautiously aware of your surroundings)— we're not looking at everybody as being a thug or a crook, but we're just being cautiously aware.

In the society in which we live, what we believe is that everyone needs to be vigilant. We should strive not to put ourselves in risky situations. If you're going shopping and will be out late, don't go by yourself. If you're walking out of the store and you see a panel van sitting next to your car, do you go out to your car? No. You go back inside and get a security officer to walk you out to your car.

Those are the types of things that I'm talking about. I believe that being cautiously aware of your environment and constantly being focused on the task at hand will help everybody.

Wright

Well, what a great conversation. It's always a pleasure talking with you, Garry. You have this subject down pat, you really have. In the speaking industry we talk about having passion for what we do. I believe you've got that passion for what you do as much as anyone I've ever seen.

Parker

I appreciate that, David.

Wright

I really thank you for taking all this time to answer these questions for me.

Today we've been talking with Garry Parker. His ability to educate, as we have found here today, makes him a delightful instructor. He uses a little southern humor to connect with each audience he speaks to. He is considered to be a leader in the prevention of school violence, workplace violence, and domestic violence.

Garry, thank you so much for being with us today on *Extreme Excellence*.

Parker

Thank you, David.

About the Author

Garry Parker has a Bachelor's Degree in Criminal Justice from Concordia University and is a Licensed Law Enforcement Trainer in Texas. Garry's ability to educate through entertainment makes him a delightful instructor. Garry uses southern humor to connect with the audience. Garry has dedicated more than 25 years to serving the people of the State of Texas as a Police Officer. After serving in enforcement for over 20 years Garry moved to the position of Public Information Education Resource Officer.

Once in the education field Garry began developing entertaining and educational presentations on topics such as traffic safety, personal safety, security and leadership. Garry has won four State awards and three National Awards for excellence in program development and presentation. Garry has served as Key Note speaker for many Local, State, National and International conferences. Garry has appeared on national television, radio, and in the national print media.

Garry is considered to be a leader in the prevention of School Violence, Workplace Violence and Domestic Violence.

Garry is a Traffic Safety consultant and has developed a Driver Safety Training Course for use by drivers of all ages in an effort to reduce crashes, injury and death.

Garry is a Certified Police Trainer in Texas and has trained literally hundreds of Police Officers.

Garry Parker
www.GarryParkerandAssociates.com

Garry Parker

Chapter 4

David Jacobson

THE INTERVIEW

David Wright (Wright)

Today we're speaking with David M. Jacobson, MSW, LCSW, author, poet, professional speaker, social worker, former college of medicine instructor, and former National Director of Training. He has been the recipient of numerous awards and honors, including a USA Book News Finalist Award for his latest book, *The 7½ Habits of Highly Humorous People*. The FlashNet Marketing President's Award, a Joy Mask from the Korean Broadcasting System, and both a Lifetime Achievement Award and a National Hero Overcoming Arthritis Award from the Arthritis Foundation. At twenty-two he was diagnosed with a severe form of arthritis that fused many of his joints and temporarily put him into a wheelchair. Ten years later he accomplished an award-winning fifty-mile unicycle ride and received the PBAA Jim Elliott Award. His purpose now is to share his discovery of how humor made his world a better place and can make the world a better place for you and those you love as well.

David, welcome to *Extreme Excellence!*

David Jacobson (Jacobson)

Thanks David, I'm glad to be here.

Wright

So what would you say would be the biggest contribution to your professional success?

Jacobson

The biggest would have to be my sense of humor. Some time ago I listened to a humorist who wasn't very humorous and it got me thinking, "Gee, I've got a great sense of humor, I should probably share it more with others, like that humorist attempted to do but failed." Even this was a positive because it motivated me to do something with my sense of humor.

In your question you used the word, "contribution," and that's an important part of the answer too because I think when I contribute to others with my humor, they feel happier, which makes me feel good that I'm contributing. This makes both of our lives richer. So contribution is also a key part of anyone's success.

One of the several common universal laws that extreme excellence involves is actually helping others, which in turn helps yourself. This is something you also know David—I know that about you. We all have unique ways that we help others and my particular one is through humor.

Wright

So what do you think are the biggest obstacles people face in trying to become successful?

Jacobson

I like that question. I really think that it is themselves, their bad habits, and their negative thoughts. My book that you mentioned, *The 7 ½ Habits of Highly Humorous People*, shows how to improve your sense of humor and by doing so how to overcome those negative thoughts. Negative thoughts create an obstacle similar to a mental brick wall. "Oh, I spilled coffee on my pants. Now the rest of the day will be ruined!" Why do we create such negative obstacles? Why don't we think that we could still have a positive, productive, successful day? This kind of thinking is a bad habit to get into and an even worse one to try to break.

Wright

What's half a habit?

Jacobson

A half habit—yeah, I get that question an awful lot. It directly relates to what I just finished saying. There actually is a half habit—it's changing negative thoughts to positive thoughts. One thing we know is we have ten of thousands of thoughts every day of our life, and they can't all be positive, so we know that we're doing some negative self-talk. This brings us down and it's not healthy. So the half habit is being able to change half of those thoughts to positive. If you can do it half the time, you're going to be twice as healthy, twice as happy, twice as sexy (I decided to throw that one in), and be just about twice as good.

Wright

Of the habits that you discuss, which one do you think is the most important habit for success and excellence?

Jacobson

That's it—the half habit is definitely the most important. As I mentioned with the coffee incident, we can have one hundred things go right before the coffee spill, yet we'll focus on that one thing that went wrong. We give more power to that than the one hundred things that went right. Successful people have a tendency to focus on what's working in their lives, not what isn't. Before that coffee spill, I got dressed and I actually fit into my pants— that was the first miracle. Then I went to work and wasn't late, another miracle. Then I made three productive calls before I poured the coffee. Finally, the coffee spills on my pants. Here comes the end of the world, negative thoughts.

Why can't I think positive instead—this spill could make a great story! I could tell everyone I was walking down the street and saw someone throwing coffee at an elderly gentleman. I quickly dived in front of him and saved his suit. This may sound silly, but if you want success and excellence in your life, using a silly, humorous, fantasy like this will drive you more toward a successful life than any negative thought. If you are able to use humor to change just half of your negative thoughts you'll be doing great.

Here are some examples of common negative thoughts and ways you can use positive or silly thoughts to counter them:

- "Nobody likes me." Change to, "I haven't met everyone yet; there's still hope."
- "My body looks gross." Change to, "Compared to what I'll look like in forty years, I don't look too bad."
- "People think I'm boring." Change to, "People who think I'm boring don't really know me—or do they?"
- "Most people are out to get me." Change to, "Most people are out to get me a gift."

I suggest readers make up some of their own that fit for them.

I would venture to guess that about 75 percent of your thoughts are negative. I base this on statistics. As we all know, 75 percent of statistics are statistically relevant. The other 25 percent fall into the category of not statistically significant or "made up." The statistic I just cited falls into the category of just "made up." That doesn't mean it may not be true though. My theory is that if you use the half habit on a daily basis you will become healthier and happier.

Wright

So in your book, *The 7½ Habits of Highly Humorous People,* you mentioned "humor spirit theory." Will you tell our readers a little more about that?

Jacobson

Humor theorists have struggled about what makes something funny ever since there have been humor theorists. Modern humor theorists have been around for over a hundred years, whereas ancient humor theorists lived in ancient times.

My Humor Spirit Theory states that humor has a spiritual aspect right from what some call the eternal soul, and it's often overlooked when being defined. Not only is there a higher power, I think there's a humor power. The basic premise of humorous spirit theory is "humorgy," a word I coined to explain that humor force. Humorgy is intuition and insight that comes from a place deep within our inner being. Just like in that movie Star Wars where they talk about "the force," there's also a humor force—a laughing force—and we feel it when we're laughing. When we laugh together with others there is a spiritual connection there. I think we feel closer to others when we share laughter together.

So my humorous spirit helps keep me going and drives me toward a more excellent and successful life. It also helps me put things into perspective and see things in a more balanced way. Most people can't have success by living alone in a cave, but helping others and others helping you is how we all become successful. Using our humorous spirit we actually accelerate the process of personal and professional development.

Wright

One example of extreme excellence from your book is your award-winning fifty-mile unicycle ride. How did your unique perspective help you accomplish this feat in spite of your severe arthritis?

Jacobson

I think it has a lot to do with this humorous spirit theory. I come from a view that success has a spirit—there's a spirit to success. That spirit of humor actually draws me toward the spirit of success. It's a feeling that you really have to experience; it's not easy to describe, but I think we've all experienced it at one time or another. We all have a drive—we all have a passion—for one or more particular things in life and my unique perspective derives from the emphasis I put on the power of humor in my life. The power of humor continually improves my life; it's the source of my love for others and myself. Extreme excellence cannot happen without feeling you deserve it, so it will obviously be a more fun experience if you're able to laugh about your success and the success of others as well.

When I was about forty miles into the ride, I was ready to quit. My knees and back felt like a dozen fishhooks were pulling on them. The wind was bone-chilling cold and blowing straight at me, almost knocking me off the unicycle. I looked up to the sky and prayed for the strength to finish. I thought of my father and his iron will and how you can do anything if you put heart and mind into it. Then I thought of all the kids with arthritis and what a great inspiration this ride could be for them. I looked to the future—to my future old age. I have four kids and I imagined my grandchildren visiting me. I had them all around the living floor in front of a fireplace and I saw myself saying, "Hey kids, did I ever tell you about the time I rode a unicycle fifty miles on a cold blustery day?" I inwardly heard the response, "Yeah Grandpa only a hundred times!" That inward smile gave me a boost. The humorous energy infused me. Humor energized my spirit. I felt my spirit's energy and continued on my way. The winds died down for a few minutes. I got my second wind (I hadn't been passing much gas) and completed the ride.

Wright

What is the message that you want people to hear so they can learn from your success?

Jacobson

If you can learn to use humor, you can overcome just about any obstacle. You can use humor to constantly teach others as well as yourself. As we know, learning and developing is a lifelong, ongoing process. Humor and laughter are recognized as so important that many professional speakers and consultants (myself included) now make a living by teaching humor skills to businesses and professional people (as well as my favorites—healthcare professionals) who want to use more humor in their speeches. So presenters and trainers especially value and use humor because it also helps their audiences to remember important points and gives their audiences a much clearer and better picture of what they want to tell them. Humor helps them retain information longer.

Wright

Do you think anyone can improve their sense of humor or are some people just naturally born funny?

Jacobson

I think anyone can improve their sense of humor, at least I hope so or my books are not going to make it as best-sellers. Seriously, some seem to be born with a natural advantage, but I think anyone can improve their sense of humor and increase their appreciation for humor. Those who do improve their sense of humor find it easier to laugh at their own mistakes and faults, making it easier for them to cope with them. That can drastically decrease the amount of stress people experience in their life. As most are aware, we can't control stress and negative events in our life, but we can control our reaction to them. A good sense of humor is one of the best ways to help us have a more healthy reaction.

Wright

What do you think is the difference between excellence and humor?

Jacobson

That's an excellent question. For me, excellence and humor coexist as two parts of the same coin. Every person's got to decide whether they're a penny or a gold piece, but we all have to value ourselves and be valuable to others. Try to use humor to see how valuable you really are and to show others how valuable they are. People who experience extreme excellence have a great sense of humor as one of their main qualities. Humor can inspire and motivate, and that in itself is where excellence comes from—inspirational humor can create excellence. If I give a powerful self-improvement message and it's also humorous, listeners are much more likely to remember it. Focused humor reinforces your most important content and the points you want to get across.

Wright

So what role does communication play in success?

Jacobson

As you may have guessed it plays a crucial role. The more you enjoy communication, the easier it is to listen and the better the message given will be remembered. As I mention in *The 7½ Habits of Highly Humorous People,* I call the best communication, co-humorcation®. This is just a word I coined that basically means communicating with humor. You can use your humorous imagination to improve your listening skills. Let's say you're angry with someone who is speaking to you. Anger will make communication very difficult, so you have to get rid of those angry feeling and moods. If you thought to yourself something like, "Well, I wonder what this person would do if cheese starting pouring out of his ear," or something silly like that, it might change your thinking. The other person might see you smile and know you're open to communication. You'll feel better and be more willing to listen—you'll be listening with humor.

Wright

So what does the most successful person you can imagine look like?

Jacobson

For me they have to be most of all highly humorous. A highly humorous person is the most resilient type of person on the planet, but humorous people learn to balance success and joy. They experience bad times, of course, just as we all do, but they put those experiences into perspective and enjoy the good times all the more. They share their humor with others.

Peak performance comes from joy. If you want to do your very best, you'll do your very best if you're enjoying the situation. So humor's your own cheerleading squad. The way that humor increases performance and improves success has only begun to be explored. I'm sure that as more and more research is done, the conclusion is going to be that humor is an integral part of success.

Wright

I find it a little bit difficult to figure out how in the world you went from being in a wheelchair to riding a unicycle for fifty miles. How in world did that happen?

Jacobson

Well, luckily I learned to ride the unicycle before I got the arthritis. My knees got so bad and my back was so bad I couldn't ride a regular bicycle anymore. I used humorous fantasy and thought, "Well, maybe I could hook another rider with a pole or get a magnet—"or something silly like that. Then I started thinking, "Well, maybe I could actually ride my unicycle." It would be a fun way to fund the arthritis foundation, which is my cause, so I hopped on a unicycle and a couple of miles later I found that I didn't have the pain in my back because I was sitting straight up. I didn't have the pain in my knees as much because the range of motion was different on the unicycle, so it actually made it easier. I was able to do my award-winning 50-mile ride and again, humor was an integral part of completing that.

Wright

That's something! Do you have any final words for our readers that would help them look at life in a little bit lighter way so their humor might help them and others?

Jacobson

I would say that you have to treat your humor as a necessity, not a luxury. I think if we hear a funny joke we kind of chuckle, but people aren't actually searching out humor or looking at humor in the same way their favorite comedian looks at it. If you treat humor as important in your life, the quality of your life can't help but improve.

Stop being so serious about everything. Celebrate being human and your gift for making mistakes. The most important lessons I've learned in my life were through making mistakes. Mistakes have improved my sense of humor, my wellbeing, and my life. I'm glad I'm not perfect—how boring and predictable would that be? Give the important things in your life the proper amount of seriousness, but give joy and laughter at least the same amount of value.

Wright

Well, what a great conversation, David. I really appreciate all the time you've spent with me today to answer all these questions. You made me think a lot differently about humor and the medicinal properties it has. I really appreciate that and sincerely want to thank you for your time.

Jacobson

Thanks for having me, I really enjoyed the conversation.

Wright

Today we've been talking with David M. Jacobson. He's an author, a poet, a professional speaker, a social worker, a former college of medicine instructor, a former National Director of Training, and he has numerous awards. One of the greatest titles of any book I've heard about is the title he has for his book, *The 7 ½ Habits of Highly Humorous People*. No wonder he has won so many awards, and no wonder he is so successful.

David thank you so much for being with us today on Extreme Excellence!

Jacobson

Thanks for thanking me and thanks for having me.

About the Author

David is a licensed clinical social worker who received his master's in social work from ASU, A BA Cum Laude in Sociology from Brockport State University and has studied at Machon Greenberg Institute in Jerusalem. He has over fifteen years of professional speaking experience and almost twenty years of psychiatric and medical social work experience. David worked several years as a hospital manager at University Medical Center, Tucson, Arizona. Appointments included: Arizona Governor's Children's Justice Task Force and Flashnet Marketing's Eagle Team which consisted of the top five national sales directors of the company. David has served as both Board President and Chair of his local chapter of the Arthritis Foundation. He also has served on the Arizona State Board of National Association of Social Workers.

Professional memberships include the Association for Applied and Therapeutic Humor and the National Speakers Association. David completed volunteer service in the VISTA/ACTION program in the United States and completed a year of volunteer service in the Israeli Civil Guard.

He has appeared in Print media, Radio and Television in the United States, and abroad.

He has been published in numerous poetry collections, was a contributing author in "Conversations on Health and Wellness along side Dr. John Gray. He is author of the award winning finalist book: *The 7½ Habits of Highly Humorous People.*

David has presented to State and Federal agencies, the military and numerous healthcare professional groups as well as the non-profits, universities and corporate sectors.

David Jacobson, LCSW
4745 S. Paseo Melodioso
Tucson, AZ 85730
520-982-6868
dj@humorhorizons.com
www.humorhorizons.com

Chapter 5

Dr. N. Elizabeth Fried

David Wright (Wright)

Today we're talking with Dr. N. Elizabeth Fried, author, consultant, and executive coach. She is also President of N.E. Fried and Associates, Inc. For twenty-five years her firm has served more than 1,500 clients worldwide. A vibrant and entertaining speaker, she addresses audiences on such topics as 360 feedback, employee engagement, and coaching. She has published two books and more than fifty professional articles. Her work has been quoted in the *Wall Street Journal, USA Today, The New York Times, The Chicago Tribune, Washington Post, US News and World Report, MS, Business Week,* and *FORTUNE Magazine.* She has also been a featured guest on over one hundred radio and television broadcasts. TheLearningEngine.org, MyExecutiveCoach.net, and Intermediaries Speaker Bureau are divisions of the firm.

Dr. Fried, welcome to *Extreme Excellence.*

N. Elizabeth Fried (Fried)

Thank you. I'm delighted to be here. I'm looking forward to our conversation. We'll be focusing on employee engagement and the Train to Ingrain® process.

Wright

So why is leadership or management training more critical today than ever before?

Fried

Basically, people quit managers, not companies. While an employee may initially join a company for its reputation, high salary, or great benefits, it's ultimately the relationship with his or her manager that keeps the employee there. So, to insure the retention of productive employees, companies need to invest in training wisely. It's a far better alternative than dealing with the staggering cost of turnover.

Let's talk specifically about how the employer/manager relationship impacts the bottom line. If we review the research on employee engagement conducted by Gallup and ISR, it reveals that operating income, net income, earnings per share, and customer satisfaction are all significantly improved when employees are engaged. Conversely, you'll find that these same areas are negatively affected when there is a *lack* of engagement. Engaged employees, for example, feel that their managers know them, are concerned about their growth and development, and really care about them. So, if we know that employee engagement increases revenues and ultimately profitability, the key question is, "Who is responsible for insuring employee engagement?" Unequivocally, it's the company's leadership.

Wright

You know, some of the people reading this book might not be as knowledgeable about employee engagement as others in the industry. Would you just simply define "employee engagement" for us?

Fried

Sure. There are three types of employees. First, you have an engaged employee. That's the person who works with passion and feels a deep connection and commitment to his or her company. This commitment is what drives innovation. They're the ones who create the momentum that thrusts the organization forward. These are the people who are critical to your organization's success to help carry out the vision, mission, and business strategy.

Then you have employees who are not engaged. These people have essentially checked out; they're often referred to as "dead men working" or "empty suits." They go through their workday putting in their time, but not their energy or passion.

Finally, we have a third group, and this is really the most destructive group—an employer's nightmare. These people are actively disengaged employees. They are unhappy at work, so they act out their dissatisfaction. I call them "pot-stirrers." They're constantly creating problems, and every day they want to subvert their engaged co-workers by distracting them with drama.

While it's critical to hire the right people—those naturally engaged employees—it doesn't stop there. Even if you do a great job of hiring the right people, then it's the leadership's responsibility to make sure that you retain these employees by sustaining their engagement. That's the key.

Wright

If strong leadership skills are so important to employee engagement and commitment, and ultimately company success, why haven't leadership programs produced the desired results?

Fried

I'll answer that with an anecdote—a familiar tale of woe. Let's say a new company started out with everyone very excited and engaged about marketing a new technology. It grows and has success. There is great camaraderie. Over time, as the company grows and new people come in, a shift occurs. It becomes clear that the company is no longer the high performing, energized team it used to be. Its managers have great technical skills, but they are lacking in the people skills required to sustain this performance. There's friction, there's tension. People are at each other's throats, morale is sinking, and sales are beginning to sag.

So top management gets together and says, "We need to do something to fix this—*fast*. Maybe we should get some leadership training to help our managers build morale and smooth things out. This seems like the solution. So they decide: If we get some training, let's hire the best! Let's make sure it's experiential and let's have great fun. We want to make sure everybody has a good time; we want to bond.

So the company goes out and spends a ton of dollars hiring this very top-rated training company, and everybody goes away for a sustained period of time, whether it's for a long weekend, a two-week retreat, or whatever. There are high expectations, but what's likely to happen? Everybody does have a good time, and they all go away thinking this was wonderful, and the training company did do a great job and got high marks. But here is the rub: In the short-term, you might see some minor change as employees carry the afterglow of the experience with them. However, a year later, you look around and you say to yourself, "What's really changed?" Regrettably, you find that people are still doing what they were doing before and not much has changed at all—SOS: Same ol' stuff.

Why don't we see any change? The primary reason is that long-lasting behavioral change is hard. No bones about it. Unfortunately, most companies have the mistaken belief that training is an event. The perception is: send people to training and *voila*—they're fixed. It's important to understand that training is *not* an event, it's a *process*. We can't just expect the training company—no matter how fabulous it is—to make the differences for us. The training company's role is to create the environment and deliver the right training. This is where most leadership programs fail—they fall into the "training is an event" trap. For real behavioral change to take place there also has to be a front-end assessment, active involvement of the participant and the participant's manager, periodic opportunities for reinforcement and coaching, and interim feedback and final measures. This is an overview of the Train-to-Ingrain process I use to insure that training sticks. This term was coined by a brilliant colleague of mine, Dr. Denny Coates, CEO of Performance Support Systems.

Wright

Will you expand on the concept of why training is a process and not an event?

Fried

I'll be happy to. It's my passion! Let's first examine how the brain works to get a clearer understanding. It's very difficult to change existing behaviors. It's much easier to learn new behaviors. When we're learning leadership skills we're not really learning new skills. For example, managers have been using their current management or leadership behaviors for years. Even though they may be using poor behaviors, they are very *good* at behaving *badly*—after all, they've been practicing for years! So, when they embark on leadership training, they're taking a maladaptive skill and attempting to turn it into an adaptive one. In order to do this, the maladaptive skill, which has been with them for years and has really been wired deeply into their brains, must be disconnected. That is the challenge and doesn't happen overnight. (Too bad we can't set blasting caps in the brain to blow out all the bad behaviors and start from scratch!)

For example, I can teach you a new skill and tell you why it is important to change your behavior. And cognitively, you know that makes sense, and you get it. But are you going to do it on a regular basis or fall back on old habitual behaviors because they are easy and comfortable?

Let's look at a very concrete example to demonstrate how this works. If I said to you, "Would you like me to show you a new way to tie your shoes so they won't come untied? And the neat thing is that you don't have to double-knot them anymore and deal with the hassle double-knotting gives you when you have to untie them."

You say to me, "Yes, Elizabeth, that sounds great. Show me."

I show it to you, you're thrilled about it, and you're so excited that you even go home and you show your significant other. Both of you think it's pretty cool. That evening you go to bed, but in the middle of the night your smoke alarm goes off. You're scrambling to get your shoes on . . . but . . . which way are you going to tie your shoes? More than likely, you'll tie them the old way. That's because changing a skill so that it's comfortable and natural requires practice, reinforcement, practice, coaching, and more practice. Tying your shoes is not a new skill. Until you disconnect the old behavior from your brain, and replace it with a skill that feels comfortable and natural, you will fall back on your own patterns when under stress. This same concept applies to management behaviors.

It's important to remember that no amateur ever made it to the pros without practice and a coach. Coaching and practice are critical to success. Let's look at Tiger Woods. Tiger was at the top of his game when he won his first Masters. He was doing really great and then he made a decision to change his swing. For those folks who follow golf, they would soon discover that Tiger Woods' game tanked as he was learning to change his swing. Why? Because often, when you're learning something new, you get worse before you get better! But, he practiced, practiced, and practiced, along with feedback and reinforcement from his coach; and he soon came back stronger than ever.

So what this indicates, in terms of leadership training programs, is that you have to structure a plan that gives learners opportunities to have lots of practice, feedback, and reinforcement. You also need to be sure that they're properly motivated by understanding where they are now by assessing their current skill levels and providing them with tools for improvement. Managers need to know employees' current skill levels and have the patience to understand that directly after training, the learners often get worse before getting better. They also need to recognize that, as managers, their role is to act as coaches to help learners improve and practice their new skills. This is a whole different way of looking at training programs. You don't want a training program that is just general and conceptual; it needs to be skill-based with opportunities for upfront measures, training, practice, reinforcement, and coaching.

Wright

So it sounds as if it's not just the people in the training department who are responsible for the success of the program, but the whole team of people. So how does one assign accountability for the different parts and then measure the success of the program?

Fried

Unfortunately, the training department has often been the scapegoat for training failures. For example, if you ask a manager, "What's your accountability in leadership training process?" Don't be surprised if you hear the manager respond, "Training is the training department's job. My job is to budget for it and arrange to get the learners' areas covered while they are away—that's all that's expected of me."

If I were Dr. Phil, I would say, "And how's that workin' for you?" The bottom line is that managers cannot take a passive role if they want training to be effective. But that is only one piece.

The process begins with a baseline measure of the employee's current skill level. I use a 360 feedback tool to gather information from the employee's manager and direct reports. I use one that is automated, simple to administer, has flexible reporting, allows for commentary, and is cost effective. This step lets people know where they are. People like to have a sense of certainty—the brain likes to have certainty because it reduces stress and frees it to learn. Brain research shows that the brain functions best when people know the expectations. So by providing a front-end assessment, the learner is given a level of certainty and expectation—this is where I am and this is where I need to be.

With assessments, we now have employees who are motivated and understand that management is working with them to get them to where they want to be. Then the training department puts together a practical, skill-based training, using appropriate adult-learning principles. The managers are informed of what the employees are going to be working on. This puts managers in a position to observe and help their employees by giving learners opportunities to practice and work on those skills. In this scenario, we've got the manager involved, having a coaching responsibility, a training department arranging for the right skill-based programs, and the employees motivated and ready to learn by an understanding of why they're going to training in the first place. Accountabilities are clearly placed.

I've seen situations where companies will send an employee to a training program and the employees are not really sure why they're going. With our Train-to-Ingrain process, it is very clear why they're going. Subsequently, the manager looks for opportunities to give them feedback, and the employee can then make improvements along the way. What the training department will do is provide additional opportunities for reinforcement by bringing in coaches and scheduling "lunch-and-learns," so people can talk about their successes and challenges on the job. These discussions are critical to the learning process as supported by brain research.

Wright

Will you elaborate more on the brain research links to leadership training?

Fried

I'll be glad to. There's been quite a bit of research with regard to the brain and how it reacts to different situations and how it learns. The common terms of "information overload" and the old adage of "I need to sleep on that," have real meaning here. Let me explain. All-day, intensive training tends to be ineffective. Spaced learning is ideal because to integrate learning, the brain needs to be able to sleep and rest. It also needs practice and reinforcement to generate and deepen neurological connections so they are firmly anchored. This means, as a trainer, information must be presented in chunks, and classes need to be shorter. More than an hour's worth of information and the brain just starts to shut down. It just can't handle it. It's like running out of RAM (random access memory) on your computer. If you want learning to stick, the new information must go from short-term memory to long-term memory. This requires periods of sleep followed by practice for reinforcement.

Let me give you a further computer analogy as it relates to behavior change. When you pull up a document in a computer, you're really operating in RAM. Any changes you make would show up on your screen, but this is really only temporary. If you don't hit the save button to make it permanent and you turn off your computer, that particular change is forever lost. To get things to save to your brain's long-term memory, you can't overload it, you need to sleep on it, and then have active practice exercises and additional feedback to reinforce it. If you don't do these things, it's like forgetting to hit the save button on your computer. It just won't stick.

Companies traditionally send people away for several days or a week of intensive training. This cost effective approach consolidates travel and minimizes work disruption. However, based on current brain research, we need to rethink our delivery methods. By developing training programs that can offer information in chunks and create opportunities for active practice and allow participants to get plenty of sleep and relaxation, behavior change is much more likely. So even though in the short-term, the Train-to-Ingrain approach is probably more costly up front, it ultimately is more cost effective in the end.

One more thing about the brain—it likes to be social and make connections among its neurons to really anchor in the new learning. As a result, you want to make sure that employees are engaged in active kinds of learning techniques along the way. By having participants talk about their experiences—their successes and their challenges—they help each other's brains to grow and connect more neurons.

Wright

Earlier you touched on assessments, skill-based training, and delivery methods to use in the Train-to-Ingrain process. What criteria should we look for when selecting assessment tools and training programs?

Fried

When doing front-end assessment, it's important to choose a 360 degree feedback platform that preserves the anonymity of the raters. This helps to insure candid feedback. The system also should allow you to customize the questions so you can measure the desired leadership skills. Additionally, you want the feedback to allow for comments because ratings alone aren't enough. Comments are often the richest part of the feedback process. However, you need to make sure that the respondents receive training on how to give behaviorally-based constructive comments. So many times I'll see reports with comments that say general things like, "He's really a great guy." Well, what does a "great guy" mean? That doesn't tell me anything. I need to know what specific behaviors a person is doing that either needs to start, stop, or continue. It is important for employees to know exactly what they need to do to perform better. (Remember, the brain likes certainty to stay calm and be open to learning.)

The system should be cost effective. That means it should allow you to do multiple surveys without additional charge. This permits interim checks and a final evaluation. Full automation and Web accessibility are critical to efficiency. The system should be easy to administer and provide well-designed reports that are uncluttered and easy to read. There are lots of good systems available today. I personally use 20/20® Insight GOLD. I find it to be one of the most robust, cost effective, efficient systems on the market. Finally, it's best to have a trained person to debrief the employee about understanding the report and creating a development plan.

When it comes to training programs, you'll want one that is practical and skill-based, using all the good adult learning principles that track with the latest brain research. As I mentioned earlier, that includes offering shorter bits of information, getting the employee engaged and interactive by involving their participation, and allowing for discussion by encouraging them to share their experiences. This technique works well with the natural brain process of seeking connections. Research shows that the brain lights up more when you are making your own connections rather than having somebody connect for you. So look for leadership programs that promote these discussion opportunities. They should also provide practice and reinforcement activities, such as roleplay and online options for a blended learning approach.

Ideally, online courses are fully integrated with the classroom content and can be used to reinforce learning through refresher activities during "lunch-and-learns" where deeper connections can be made through ongoing dialogue. Then six months to nine months after the training is complete, do a reassessment of that person and see how he or she has improved. This step will let you know what's working and where the person may need some additional coaching, training, or reinforcement. You may determine that the person really doesn't belong in a leadership role and would be more effective as an individual contributor. All of that is important information and contributes to the learning loop.

So it's the combination of a front-end assessment and good adult learning principles, such as practice and reinforcement, which are critical for your success.

Another very important aspect of the classroom training is that you not only need to provide practical skills, but you also have to give participants opportunities for role-modeling and roleplaying to practice those skills. So look for programs that show the right behavior using very brief, professionally developed video or DVD scenarios. Then break the group into triads to practice these skills. These triads involve one person acting as the observer, another taking the role of the employee, and another becoming the manager. Allow for a two- to three-minute roleplay, and then have them swap roles. Now the employee becomes the observer, the observer becomes the manager, and so on, so they all get a chance to function in each capacity and continue to practice the new skills. All participants experience the skill in action to help them apply it on the job. Then several weeks later, during a reinforcement activity, such as a lunch-and-learn, they can discuss how it's been working for them.

Wright

So let me see if I can understand this Train-to-Ingrain program you have. The main challenge is to permanently replace a maladaptive skill with an adaptive skill by hardwiring the brain to create long-lasting behavioral change, right?

Fried

Absolutely; you've got it. That's it in a nutshell.

Wright

And the Train-to-Ingrain methodology is designed to shift and spread the accountability to insure the learner is motivated and the right skills are being trained and reinforced.

Fried

That's right. We have the learners who will come to class motivated because they now are clear about expectations and why they need to improve on new skills. They've gotten feedback from their managers and direct reports about what behaviors need to be continued, stopped, or changed. This information helps them capitalize on their strengths and work on their development.

The role and responsibility of the training department is to provide the right kind of training resources and environment. Finally, the manager's role is to offer coaching, reinforcement, and support to the employee. All three—the manager, training department, and employee—are now accountable for a clearly defined piece of the program.

Wright

What an interesting concept. And the recent brain research seems to support the methodology.

Fried

Absolutely. One of the programs that I use is an award-winning series published by Vital Learning. It is a skill-based, practical program that employs solid adult learning principles. For example, in its "Essential Skills of Leadership Module," it addresses the importance of building and maintaining an employee's self-esteem. Esteem-building is critical to employee engagement and backed by current brain research.

I find this part of the brain research particularly fascinating. It shows that if an employee is berated by his or her manager, the brain reacts in a very interesting way. It starts producing cortisol, which is naturally created during stress situations. When under a stress situation, the place where memory is stored (the hippocampus) starts to shrink. This reduces the production of neurons that affect memory, mood, and other mental functions. As a result, the brain doesn't think clearly or perform well. (Probably because primitive man was designed to react in stress or fear situations to fight or flee, not think!)

Conversely, if an employee is made to feel valued, then the brain produces serotonin, and the employee feels better. This condition allows the employee's mind to be open to change and learning as well as be more supportive of his or her manager, making the relationship with that manager even stronger. A strong relationship with one's manager, as I mentioned in the very beginning of our conversation, is a key factor in insuring employee engagement and retention.

This research is not only interesting from a neurological standpoint, but also directly connects to learning and engagement.

To recap, the lessons that we learn from neuroscience is that people need to have sleep so they can integrate learning into long-term memory because the brain shuts off after a period of time. Learning needs to be broken down into bite-sized nuggets. Social pain—being rejected or berated—has an impact on the brain the same way that physical pain does. So if someone feels social pain, such as being berated, the brain lights up similarly to when it is experiencing physical pain. If the manager berates the employee or treats the employee poorly, this is not going to be helpful. Social fairness and respect provide good chemicals in the brain, while unfairness and disrespect create just the opposite of that. If you're overly stressed because of fear of uncertainty, you're not going to be able to think clearly, and, your mind is likely to shut down.

So, for example, in these training programs, leaders need to give employees appropriate performance expectations and communicate the vision of the organization so they know where they're going. They need a road map. If employees feel uncertain, then this arouses fear, and fear reduces their ability to make good decisions.

Additionally, employees also need to have some kind of involvement or ownership of their particular situation in the organization so that they can contribute on a greater level and make brain connections. Having some choice enables their brain to function more openly, allowing it to be more insightful. All of these factors are interconnected and contribute to the learning process.

Wright

This seems to be a real advancement of the old learning model that I learned in the fifties, and especially the model that came out in the early seventies. They called it "spaced repetition."

Fried

Spaced repetition is still a part of it, which comes in the form of practice, but is only one component.

Wright

Interesting. I really appreciate all the time you've taken with me today to answer these questions. It's not only fascinating but I've learned a lot here that I'm going to think a whole lot about. I've taken copious notes. I really do appreciate your being with us today.

Fried

Thank you. Seeing people achieve success is my passion, so it was my pleasure being with you today.

Wright

Today we've been talking with Dr. Elizabeth Fried. She is an author, consultant, and executive coach. She is a vibrant and entertaining speaker, as we have found out here today. She has addressed audiences on topics such as 360 feedback, executive coaching, and employee engagement.

Dr. Fried, thank you so much for being with us today on *Extreme Excellence.*

About the Author

Dr. N. Elizabeth Fried, author, consultant, and executive coach, is president of N.E. Fried and Associates, Inc. For the past twenty-five years, her firm has served more than 1,500 clients worldwide. A vibrant, entertaining, and informative speaker, she is frequently invited to speak on such topics as 360 feedback, employee engagement, and coaching. Her first book, Outrageous Conduct: Bizarre Behavior at Work, was a Society of Human Resource Management best-seller, followed by its sequel, Sex, Laws, and Stereotypes. Her work has been quoted in the *Wall Street Journal, USA Today, The New York Times, The Chicago Tribune, Washington Post, US News and World Report, MS, Business Week,* and *FORTUNE Magazine.* She has also been a featured guest on over one hundred radio and television broadcasts. TheLearningEngine.org, MyExecutiveCoach.net, and Intermediaries Speaker Bureau are divisions of the firm.

N. Elizabeth Fried, PhD
7564 Romeria St.
Carlsbad, CA 92009
760-633-4444
elizabeth@TheLearningEngine.org
www.TheLearningEngine.org
www.MyExecutiveCoach.net

Chapter 6

Rick Cooper

David Wright (Wright)

Today we're talking with Rick Cooper, The Sales Results Expert. He is author of *Million Dollar Contacts* and co-author of *Marketing Magic.* He is a national speaker on sales results and sales productivity. Rick is Founder and President of The PDA Pro, which specializes in helping small business owners attract clients and grow their business. Rick coaches and trains his clients to increase their sales results by improving their sales skills, increasing their sales productivity, and leveraging technology tools. He was featured in *Comstock's Magazine* and has been interviewed for national publications. Rick shares advice on his blog and Internet radio show titled *Attracting Ideal Clients.*

Rick, welcome to *Extreme Excellence.*

Rick Cooper (Cooper)

Thank you David. It's a pleasure to join you for this interview.

Wright

Small business owners typically have too much on their plate. What advice do you have to build a business based on excellence?

Cooper

First of all, David, I have a lot of respect for small business owners. They work very hard and take a lot of risks to build a successful business.

There are two key qualities to become successful. First, you must focus your efforts on worthwhile and productive activities that will help you achieve your goals. You can't be everything to everybody. You have to set goals and limit your commitments. It's so critical to stay on target. The second quality is persistence. There are many obstacles on the road to success. To achieve excellence, you must be persistent. You have to keep working toward your goals even when the road gets rough. Strive to be better and offer excellent service to your clients. Be flexible and make adjustments when needed.

My desire to start my own business began in college. I've always loved to read books on business, and in college I had the opportunity to join and then later become president of a business club called The Entrepreneurial Network. We invited entrepreneurs from the business community to speak to students. Meeting entrepreneurs face-to-face sparked a passion for entrepreneurship and inspired me to start my own business. Later, I had the opportunity to become President of the Arden Lunch Chapter of TNI, The Network. I love small businesses and I'm passionate about coaching small business owners to reach their goals and accomplish more.

Wright

What do you suggest for business owners who want to grow their business and increase their sales results?

Cooper

One thing to keep in mind is that "sales" is a skill. It's one of the most challenging skills to master. You can always improve your results. Make an effort to learn something new about sales every month and develop your sales skills. Remember that the sales process is simply a tool to help you serve people and provide solutions for their problems.

I mentioned the importance of setting goals earlier. I can't emphasize enough the importance of setting business goals, especially sales goals. If you want to grow your business, then you have to create an intention or an expectation of the results that you want. This allows you to measure your performance and improve your results.

I offer a free resource called the Sales Results Success Kit, available at SalesResultsKit.com. You'll receive tips and strategies to increase your sales results. Being able to focus on the bottom line is important. In order to grow your business, it's critical to set your sales goals and then work toward achieving them.

Wright

What strategies do you recommend for people who run a home-based service business?

Cooper

Many of the people who start a business offer some kind of professional service to others. They have a technical skill and they want to serve others. Working from home makes a lot of sense. It allows you to keep your overhead low and balance the needs of work and family. It can also create a number of challenges. Interruptions and distractions can cause you to procrastinate and avoid working on your top priorities.

If you want to be more successful, then you have to work smarter, not harder. And that starts with setting daily priorities. You have to connect to your goals and choose activities that will move you in the direction of success.

Establish a regular schedule and let people know when you're available. You can get more done in less time by batching common activities.

My clients often mention they feel more productive and effective after working with me.

Finally, you have to create a boundary between your work and home life to find balance and reduce stress. This will improve your personal and your professional relationships. I recommend you build your business around your life and not the other way around. Your business shouldn't be a burden.

Wright

What are some of the common challenges small business owners have in finding their ideal clients?

Cooper

First, let's consider why a small business owner would even want to find their ideal clients. One common mistake people make is thinking anyone is a prospective client. Not everyone is the perfect customer for you, and this is especially true for service businesses. Do you really want to work with people you don't really like or care about? Do you want to work with people who don't appreciate your services? You'll have much better results and can charge more if you identify the best people for you to work with.

Ask yourself the following questions to identify your ideal clients:
- What industry are they in?
- What is their income level?

- Where are they located?
- What groups do they belong to?
- What are their hobbies and interests?

When you identify your ideal clients, it's much easier to attract them. One way people limit themselves is choosing to work only with people in their local area. This is playing small. Instead, play big! Get your message out nationally and globally to attract your ideal clients. It doesn't have to cost a fortune.

Wright

What technology tools do you recommend to help them find more clients?

Cooper

Two of the most common sales tools are contact management systems and PDA/smartphones, also called personal digital assistants. It's absolutely essential to enter information about your clients and prospects, schedule appointments, and track tasks. Technology tools can help you to stay in integrity. There are also many technology tools that can help you attract clients including e-mail marketing tools, which enable you to send e-mail announcements and an e-zine (electronic-magazine). You can build a Web site, post to a blog, and connect with people through social networks and other social media sites. That's why it's so important to select a niche. When you narrow your focus, it's much easier to find your ideal clients. You will find it easier to understand their needs and find a way to serve them. (I share more details in a free audio called "7 Steps to Attract your Ideal Clients," available at www.AttractClientsAudio.com.)

Imagine two business owners, one who builds his or her business locally and the other who builds his or her business nationally. Who's going to succeed? It depends on how well owners have identified their ideal clients and what actions they have taken to communicate their value proposition. Ultimately, either one can be more successful, but business owners who choose to market business nationally will have a better chance of reaching their ideal clients. They will be able to use strategies that will pinpoint their ideal clients and allow them to speak to them directly with a targeted message. And that's powerful!

Wright

So what does it mean to be excellent in sales?

Cooper

I think the true measure of success in sales is based on the service you provide. It starts with understanding your clients' needs and finding the best way to serve them. It's not about pushing a product, but understanding what they need and finding a way to serve them even if it doesn't involve making a sale. It's a long-term view of success.

Sales excellence also means setting and achieving sales goals and that starts with understanding the relationship between activities and results. If you know your closing ratio, then you know how many appointments you need in order to make a sale. That will help you determine how many calls you need to make every day to schedule appointments. Sales is a repeatable process. You have to take action consistently to achieve excellence. You'll also find that sales come more easily when you consistently take action. You create momentum and break down the fears that hold you back.

Wright

So what are some of the ways to build a referral business based on excellence?

Cooper

If you own a service business, then you know that referrals are essential to attracting clients. It starts with communicating a consistent, compelling message to your clients and prospects. Your message should identify your ideal clients and how you help them. The key is to plant a seed someone will remember and that will inspire the person to refer you. You have to ask for referrals. Let your clients know that you depend on referrals to grow your business and you want more clients like them.

Be sure to thank clients when they refer others to you. Send them a thank you card or a gift. If they have sent you several referrals, take them to lunch to build your relationship with them.

Don't overlook the importance of providing a high level of service. Keep your promises and over-deliver. You need testimonials from people who love your services. Ask for testimonials in writing and make sure that it paints a picture of what things were like before and after they worked with you. Results matter!

Wright

What tips do you have for entrepreneurs who want to increase their sales productivity and become more effective?

Cooper

Sales productivity is a critical factor in your success. It's one of the areas where I work with my clients. After all, I am "The PDA Pro." PDA stands for Productivity, Discipline, and Action. You can increase your productivity if you exercise discipline and take action.

Three key areas to improve your productivity:
- Habits—Improve your personal habits
- Organization—Get organized
- Technology—Leverage technology tools

Improve your personal habits, get organized, and leverage technology tools, and you'll increase your productivity. But you have to remember that productivity is only one piece of the puzzle. You also have to be effective. You can be very productive doing busy work and it will do nothing for your overall effectiveness. As an entrepreneur, it's easy to procrastinate and spend too much time pushing pencils and paper.

My father taught me at a young age the importance of working on important tasks. You need to get very clear about what activities are important in finding and serving clients. This is one of the areas where I hold clients accountable. It's important to make sure they spend the majority of their time working on their top priorities. Finally, use a calendar to block out time for important activities. Prioritize your actions and focus on high value activities.

Wright

Will you tell our readers some of the myths about productivity?

Cooper

One of the current myths about productivity is that multitasking is an effective use of your time. In most cases multitasking is simply a distraction. You will be far more effective if you block out time to focus on a single activity. If you need to make sales calls, then clear everything off your desk, pull out your call list, pick up the phone, and start making calls. Make sure that you close your e-mail and eliminate other distractions that will take you off track.

One other surprising disadvantage of multitasking is that it reduces your creativity. That's because you don't really multitask. You simply work on multiple tasks and jump back and forth. It lowers your ability to concentrate. If you need to do something creative like write an article, book, or Web site copy, it's much easier if you can sit down and focus your energy and effort. That will allow you to focus creatively and get the job done quickly and easily. Focus like a laser!

Wright

So many service professionals get burned out in their professions, since delivering their services depends so much on their time. What can they do to spend more time *on* their business rather than just *in* their business?

Cooper

Great question David. Once you grow your business to a certain point, you may find it necessary to delegate certain responsibilities. Focus on your strengths and delegate the rest. Find an employee whose skills compliment yours. Look for someone who is strong in an area where you are weak. Hire a virtual assistant who can support you. Michelle Ulrich, Founder of The Virtual Nation, says you will be far more effective when you can clear a few things off your plate so you can focus on your most important activities. This will also unleash your creativity.

Many small business owners think they can just hire someone else to sell for them. This is a mistake. As the business owner, you will always be the most effective person when it comes to finding clients. You have the credibility and the passion to communicate your value proposition effectively. Once your business is successful, then it may be time to hire a sales professional. Until you reach that point, work on yourself and improve your sales skills. Take a class, attend a teleseminar, or work with a sales results coach. Learn how to improve your marketing. Enlist the help of others to spread your message. Build relationships with people who have a large sphere of influence.

Eric Lofholm, sales scripting expert and Master Sales Trainer, calls this the Person of Influence (POI) strategy. A POI is a person with a large network where a percentage of that network is your target market. This person can endorse you and enhance your credibility with people in his or her circle of influence.

It's also important to build balance into your life. Take at least one day off every week. Don't work on that day—just take time to rest and relax. If you are spiritual, then spend time in reflection and prayer. Volunteer and help others. Cultivate friendships outside of the business arena. Become a well-rounded person. This will contribute to your success.

Wright

That makes a lot of sense, Rick. What steps should small business owners take to become more successful?

Cooper

There are several critical steps to build a successful business. You need to create a business plan, set goals, and measure your results. Make sure you take time to learn new skills and improve your sales and marketing. It's important to implement new strategies to increase your sales results. Make sure that you identify your ideal clients and look for ways to attract them. Find ways to create value for others and look for ways to serve them.

Ian Selbie, Founder of Conselleo, a leading sales management consulting firm, says that creating strategic value is critical to consultative selling. You need to become a problem-solver and have a variety of solutions.

Find a coach or a mentor you can work with. I have worked with five coaches since I started my business in May 2003. Each one helped me in a different area to get the results I wanted. Look for someone who will challenge you and hold you accountable.

David, most entrepreneurs struggle on a daily basis. They're just working to survive. I have a message of hope for them: you can have a better life! You just have to take action every day to improve what you are doing.

Andrew Barber-Starkey, Master Certified Coach and Founder of ProCoach International, suggests celebrating all of the little successes in your life and your business. That will increase your confidence and motivate you to persist and succeed. Create a network of people you have met or spoken with and follow up with them over time. Feed your network. Stay in touch and ask them what they're working on. Look for ways to help. Be sincere and authentic. People can sense the true nature of your character. If you are truly authentic and sincere, then people will go out of their way to help you. I have found that to be true in my own life. Finally, do your best and strive for excellence.

Wright

I think you hit it on the spot. Being an entrepreneur, I have found it sometimes to be a lonely job.

Cooper

It's easy to get stuck when you focus too much on yourself.

Wright

But then I found out I couldn't be an isolationist and an entrepreneur at the same time.

Cooper

You're absolutely right, David. Success is a team sport. The key is to look for people in your life who can help you. There are so many different ways you can connect with people. I mentioned some of the strategies earlier about writing a blog, sending an e-zine, or joining an online social network. Those are all ways you can connect with other people. Build relationships with others and give advice or share ideas. Look for ways to help them. This will create very powerful relationships. This is not limited to contractual relationships. Create relationships where you're both working toward a similar goal. Hold each other accountable.

I have a great relationship with social media expert Jerry Hart, author of *Blueprint to eMarketing*. We became friends first and now focus on the outcomes of working together. That's the benefit of a joint venture or a strategic alliance. Make it a priority to find alliance partners and work together to help each other find and serve clients. This is one of the joys in business.

Wright

Great advice, Rick. As a matter of great conversation, I'm listening to you more often now, and these principles are actually helping me. I appreciate it. What a great conversation, Rick. I always enjoy talking with you and I really appreciate the time you've taken to answer these questions. You really know what you're doing.

Cooper

Thanks, David. The topic of excellence is such a great one because it really gets to the heart of the matter. It's about creating a powerful, successful life. It's about learning to step into your greatness. It's about learning to achieve your goals and build the life of your dreams.

Wright

Today we've been talking with Rick Cooper, The Sales Results Expert. Rick is Founder and President of The PDA Pro, which specializes in helping small business owners attract clients and grow their business. His clients increase their sales results by improving their sales skills, increasing their sales productivity, and leveraging technology tools.

Rick Cooper

Rick, thank you so much for being with us today on *Extreme Excellence.*

Cooper

You're welcome, David. It's been my pleasure. Thank you.

About the Author

Rick Cooper is The Sales Results Expert. He specializes in helping small business owners attract clients and grow their business. Rick is Founder and President of The PDA Pro. As an author, a speaker, and coach, he helps entrepreneurs achieve outstanding results. He teaches people to leverage technology tools to follow up consistently and increase their sales results through his Sales Results Success Program.

Rick is author of *Million-Dollar Contacts*, a contact management guide. He is co-author of *Marketing Magic*, which provides innovative tips on marketing, sales, and public relations. He shares strategies to follow up effectively through his audio program "Fortune is in the Follow-Up: 7 Surefire Strategies to Turn Prospects into Repeat Clients."

Rick is a national speaker on Sales Results and Sales Productivity. He was featured in *Comstock's* magazine and has been interviewed by *The National Networker, AllBusiness.com,* the *Get More Business Podcast,* and the *East Bay Times Business Journal.* Rick is also a blogger, podcaster, and Internet radio show host.

Rick is a partner with Conselleo, a leading sales management consulting firm, a Master Teacher in sales for the University of Masters and a coach for Eric Lofholm International, Inc.

He has held roles including President of the Arden Lunch Chapter of TNI, Program Chair of the Management Consultants of Sacramento, and Ambassador of the Sacramento Metro Chamber of Commerce.

Rick S. Cooper, MBA
The Sales Results Expert
President, The PDA Pro
3323 Watt Avenue, #280
Sacramento, CA 95821
800.677.6708
Rick@ThePDApro.com
www.ThePDApro.com

Chapter 7

Angeline Teo

David Wright (Wright)

Today, I'm talking with Angeline V. Teo. She is Founder and Principal Consultant of d'Oz International Pte Ltd, a professional learning and development solutions provider based in Singapore. She has acquired a wealth of experience through coaching senior executives, working with diverse cultures, and managing collaborations with multinationals, education, and government Institutions in Asia-Pacific, and Europe.

She is a Master Trainer and an Accredited consultant with PEPWorldwide in Asia-Pacific, and a Certified Career Coach with WorkLife Asia. Her trademarked formula, SPAM (Stay Positively Active and Motivated) and CCQ (Cross-Cultural Quotient) have made her a regular contributor and feature on various major print, radio, and television media in the Asia-Pacific.

Her thoughts and experiences in the travel industry are being echoed by her published articles on leading travel and MICE publications (Meeting Incentives Conventions and Exhibitions) including MiceAsia.net, *Frequent Traveller, TTG Asia, Tiger Tales, The Finder Singapore.*

She has also been on the pages of *Straits Times, Today's Manager, Human Resource, Entrepreneur's Digest, Frequent Traveller* and women's magazines such as *Shape and HerWorld,* sharing gained knowledge on being a successful entrepreneur, a employee-friendly employer, and even an effective and efficient worker.

Angeline, tell me about the turning moment or event in your life that brought you to the path of coaching and speaking.

Angeline V. Teo (Angeline)

Passion to making a difference in life is by choice, not by chance.

Over twenty-five years of experience in the corporate world has paved the way for great opportunities. My frequent business and leisure trips around the world gave me a lot of exposure—priceless moments of seeing the whole world in distinct, beautiful perspectives, getting more accustomed to different people and culture, developing my skills, and undergoing training conducted by many top gurus and experts in the field of management, sales, marketing, and communications. And most important of all, by experiencing the inevitable harsh realities and difficulties brought about by this journey, I have learned the value of change opportunities that we must find to make things better and make life more manageable and easy to deal with.

When I was managing and leading teams of salespeople and developing the business in the travel industry, I often came up with new ideas on how I can continuously motivate, encourage innovation, and empower my teams. I was on the other side; I was engaging speakers to add flavor to the simple entertainment luncheons, which were easily put together. The "new" approach then was very well received by the travel agents and corporate clients whom I invited. I recalled getting Nancy Ho, a petite and yet dynamic speaker, who got everyone so engrossed in her presentation that each time we met, my clients would be asking for more of such sessions and talking about it! The results led me to be bolder with my marketing expenditures and I started one-day workshops, followed by two-day workshops as incentives for my top performing clients. It was meaningful and it was fun!

All the objectives were met:
1. The sales team members got a chance to build rapport with their clients during the workshops.
2. Clients were looking forward to the next event and motivated to continue supporting us.
3. Everyone walked out learning something new and valuable.
4. It was money well spent for me, as the Sales Manager.

I was inspired each time I heard a new speaker. It may be on the topic of Leadership, Creativity, Sales, or Projecting a Professional Image. Every session took me to the next level, thinking, "I want to be there, on the other side, to inspire, to make a difference in someone's business and life."

The feelings got stronger and stronger by the day. I walked up to Nancy one day and said, "I want to be like you."

I started consciously searching for opportunities to hone my skills in speaking and enhance my knowledge. I may have had many years of experience, however, it just was not enough if I wanted to excel. I must continuously read more, listen more, travel more, speak more, and ask more. I was always accepting invitations by Colleges, Polytechnics, and institutions to speak for free. They were like test-beds for me. I wanted to know if I was ready to give up the corporate life and go into the jungle of the unknown territory.

Between 2001 and 2003 people were recovering from the aftermath of world calamities—the Bali bombing, the 9/11 attack of World Trade Center in the United States, the SARS outbreak, and a big population of people who lost their jobs in Singapore.

I was a victim in 2002. Perhaps it was the Law of Attraction that was working up on me! Remember, I was already visualizing my speaking career, up on stage in front of hundreds and thousands of people, and enjoying every moment of it. I was passionate about it. I needed a jump master to push me over . . . and it happened!

In August 2002, I took the ultimate risk of investing my "retrenchment package" in a business endeavor, now d'Oz International, the leading learning and development organization.

I only knew then that I wanted to make a difference in people's lives. I worked hard to improve my speaking skills; I enrolled in Master Trainers' programs and became accredited to be a Coach. I joined Speakers Network and served the members for a few years. I joined a coaching network and a few associations to expand my horizon. I attended as many seminars, conferences, and events as I possibly could to learn from world gurus and specialists. I was passionate and I was serious about sharing my experience, delivering knowledge and values to my audience through coaching, and speaking.

The setting of d'Oz International in 2002 was an excellent platform for me to extend a helping hand, especially to those who were desperately seeking consolation and guidance to get back on their feet. The situation was tense in Singapore, as each day we were plagued by news of how many companies went out of business and people would lose their jobs. Sad stories were spread across the dailies. I constantly thought about how I could put my experience and knowledge into their best use and to reach out to as many people as quickly as possible. People were desperate because jobs were scarce.

Together with a partner speaker, we put together a series of free seminars to inspire and to motivate those who had lost their jobs. We gave them hope and shared with them some tips on how to start small businesses and to regain their dignity and self-confidence again. Since I was a victim in 2002—I lost my job too—I was able to empathize, and the audience listened, and they did listen attentively as they witness the positive energy I was reflecting across the room to each and every one of them. Many of them lined up after each session to speak with me and to thank me for giving them hope. It was heartwarming to just hear them say so.

The series of six sessions over a couple of months in 2003 concluded successfully with new hope and smiles on the faces of over 2,000 people. We felt good. I felt good. We were thankful to the companies that helped us by sponsorship of the hotel function rooms, for the venue, and food. We even had free publicity and promotions from the country's largest transportation service provider, SMRT (Singapore Mass Rapid Transport).

I never looked back. I knew that was my calling—it's my purpose in this journey to make a difference in someone's life through speaking and coaching.

Wright

How fulfilling and unique is coaching and speaking as a career compared to other professions?

Angeline

"You will never have to work another day if you learn the skills to efficiently enjoy what you are doing today."

It's a calling, not just another profession. If you do it for the money alone, you will fail badly. If you do it from the heart with passion, it's extremely fulfilling and rewarding.

You must have the passion and desire to see people benefit. This will actually outweigh the monetary returns you will reap. However, we cannot discount the fact that we still need financial resources to be able to expand, to upgrade, and to reach out to more people, to improve their work and life conditions.

I had one experience with a very high profile lady who approached me to help coach her for an impending presentation. She needed to build her confidence to stand in front of an audience of over eight hundred people in an upcoming corporate event. She was invited to give an opening speech and she had this thing called fear of embarrassment. She beat herself up with these negative thoughts and had been getting sleepless nights before she met with me. She would constantly self-talk, "What if I fumble? What if I forget my lines? What if I embarrass myself?"

In the past, I had always thought that only those who held senior positions such as high-profile CEOs should be able to carry themselves very well at corporate events. I was wrong. The coaching session I had with her, just three times over one month, had given her the courage and skills to deliver her speech confidently. She thanked me, even offering me more than I had quoted her!

We all know that speaking in front of an audience is the greatest fear for most people; even greater than the fear of death. However, once you work with a coach to learn the skills to take control of your breathing, delivery and tonality, you will gain confidence and even look forward to the next.

When I witness the positive change and the progress made by each client, I feel more inspired to do better for more people. The speaking opportunities help me to fulfill this gap because it reaches masses faster, encouraging them to peak their performance and keep balance between their work and life.

Wright

What are the distinctive lessons you get from being a speaker and coach?

Angeline

"There is always another mountain higher than this other one"—adapted from a Chinese proverb. It means, "There will always be someone who will be smarter and better than you."

I am humbled by the many events of life that took place during my international journey of speaking and coaching. I have learned how to unlearn and re-learn new things, to be always on the lookout for new experiences, and be able to share joyfully with others through, of course, the coaching and speaking sessions. These are the small things that we take for granted. We sometimes cannot see the value of the impact that these small things can make on other people. Seeing someone learn new things and lending a hand to others are indeed joyful moments.

Coaching equates to the learning process. The power of the mind is crucial for the success of the individual. It is the attitude that determines the altitude in one's life. Learning is about doing more than knowing—apply what you have learned by doing and sharing it with others. Coaching helps people to put into action what they seek to achieve. And that makes coaching and learning a very dynamic profession and process.

I enjoy the journey of coaching and speaking, respect cultural differences, I deepen my learning of each industry, and constantly innovate new approaches that will help my clients in achieving their quests to be successful, be it in business or personal.

To be a professional speaker and a coach needs a lot of conscious and continuous effort in staying relevant. It requires keeping abreast of the ever-changing economy, and most importantly, providing quality delivery.

To progressively improve in what I am doing and to upgrade myself, I will:

1. self-coach through self-exploration to achieve greater fulfillment in what I am doing;
2. pray and reflect daily—morning and evening;
3. set questions for myself to challenge my thinking;
4. find opportunities to spar with fellow speakers to feed my inquisitive mind;
5. observe the environment to understand the changes;
6. seek alignment with my life purpose and values;
7. walk the talk to also make time for my family and friends to achieve a work-life balance;
8. read, listen, research, get help;
9. continuous life-long learning;
10. take care of my health; enjoy and have fun.

Wright

Behind successful people are their own coaches or advisors. Who are your mentors? Do you have a separate mentor for personal and professional matters?

Angeline

The big secret to becoming successful is to learn from the mistakes others have made and be willing to make a change for the better from the latter's experiences.

I give credit to a lot of people and experiences that have influenced me professionally and personally. My parents are my greatest personal mentors. They have inculcated the values of life and have walked beside me through life's obstacle race. My spouse, who has shared the second half of my journey, is also my mentor. There are other people who have touched and inspired me. Dr. Mel Gill is one of the first persons who had coached and prepared me to follow my heart. The late Tony D'Arcy inspired me to carry my torch and be strong. Other brilliant coaches include Denis Healy, Mark Holden and Shelley Sykes.

There are also those people who outgrew hardships and managed to find the path en route to success. I regard them as role models in my life. One such person is Olivia Lum, CEO and Founder of Hyflux in Singapore. Her story has touched me greatly. She was an orphan who took the initiative to study. Because of her ingenuity and right attitude, she was propelled to live a better life. She is a believer in the fact that everything is possible. She did not make her pitiful situation an excuse to give up; rather, she took it as a challenge to achieve greater heights.

For all those people who have inspired me and coached me directly or indirectly, I thank them for their guidance.

Professionally, I am blessed with having many successful business partners and speaker friends from whom I can seek advice and exchange ideas together. A famous Chinese proverb says, "There will always be another mountain higher than this other." This is an analogy that means there will always be someone who is wiser and more knowledgeable than you are.

As I continue my journey in speaking and coaching, I will find new masters through the books that are written, through the speeches that are made and through the discussions that are held. Each one is a hero in their own right. They have given inspiration, taught new knowledge, introduced new techniques, and showed new ways. They are my mentors. They are generous to share and to provide advice when I need it.

I take personal responsibility in constantly making time to read journals, articles, and stories of "unsung heroes" to add to my personal library. This will feed my knowledge bank so that I can in turn share them with my clients, and to showcase the "heroes." From this exercise, I find new mentors and advisors along this exciting journey on which I embark.

Wright

What was the first success in your life? How about the first failure? How did you deal with those life-altering circumstances?

Angeline

The old adage, "Failure is the mother of all successes" still stays with me, and I am sure, with many other successful people too. It helps to bring us back to perspective on what life is built upon—the lessons learned from each experience of failures during our journey in search of success.

I must say, my first experience of success was when I gave birth to my eldest daughter. As a woman, the pinnacle of my success is being able to bring forth another life and to raise her the best way I know. She is now over eighteen years old and we are very close to each other. I constantly look back and recollect that wonderful experience of first-time motherhood. I now have two beautiful daughters, Sherrianne and Cherylanne, age eighteen and fifteen years respectively.

I have encountered many first failures in life—yes, many first failures of differing natures. Two of the most unforgettable ones include the failure to launch the first franchise business venture with a Singapore government link organization to operate a school in China. My business partners and I were so eager to secure a venture into China that we over-rated the capability of the franchisor. The operation in China, unfortunately, never took off because we were not able to secure a license to operate, despite our franchisor's supposedly renowned reputation in Singapore; the latter's license submission was rejected in China. Hence, an investment of over $350,000 in relationship-building, training, personal development, and infrastructures were lost. We have learned our lessons from here on to be more cautious when seeking business partnerships.

The second is the failure of my first marriage. I was only twenty-four when I got married after an eight-year courtship. I thought I was ready. I was never taught about how to manage the increasing demand of managing a family and the pressure of carving a career for myself then. I focused on the latter, attending night classes after work to build up my professional portfolio. I traveled extensively to attend to duty calls. I was ambitious. I was putting in 99 percent of my time at work because I did not have children then. I did neglect to pay attention by my spouse, pushing attention to him aside as an unreasonable demand. We failed to communicate and that drew us further and further apart. We were aliens to each other and we could tolerate each other no longer after seven years. We parted in 1996, ending in an acrimonious divorce.

I have accepted these experiences wholeheartedly. I have taken them as drivers of learning, development, and change. As I look back and remember the experiences I have had, I just smile and sometimes laugh at how I showed naiveté and ignorance toward different circumstances. So, don't be hard on yourself—failures and mistakes are part of life experiences.

However, once erring becomes a habit, it's a hard habit to break, and then it's a fact that you are taking things passively, evading learning and improvement.

I've dealt with success and failures in a positive way, as we always should. Charge every mistake to experience and you'll be amazed by the astounding learning that will show you how to prevent a situation from happening again. Take every opportunity to help other people. Share stories about how you failed, coped with the failure, and managed to eventually succeed. Think about it—many people like Albert Einstein failed hundreds or maybe even thousands of times before they were satisfied that they were successful.

A mature and successful person realizes that there are a lot of things to learn and to explore. Live life actively and do things extraordinarily. A quick pick me-up-line is to, "Stay Positive, Active, and Motivated" (SPAM). That will get you to look at things from a different perspective and to bounce back from any challenges in life.

Wright

What is your inspiration behind the advocacy of work-life balance, cross-cultural intelligence (quotient), and "career womanhood"? How relevant are these topics in today's society and corporate environment?

Angeline

The best inspiration is when you know you have everything to lose if you do not give it another try again and again.

Losing control over time, as I lived from day to day without focusing on the quality of living, I realized that my children were growing up so quickly. I was missing out on some of the activities I would have enjoyed with them. I should have known that an imbalance in time allocated between work and personal life would affect not only me but more on the people close to my heart. Fortunately, I realized soon enough the importance of being with my children during their growing up years. Seeing how my daughters had benefitted from my close involvement in their personal growth and development, I was determined to not only continue learning about work-life balance to further improve our lives, but to also be an advocate to help other people with the knowledge I had gained.

Today, amid the advancements in information technology, increasing workflow, events of mergers and acquisitions, increasing stress and burnout levels, and high attrition rate, we lack the appropriate knowledge to deal with these things. We know how to be experts in our own fields; however, we are poor in managing life and workload. This is a conclusion made by efficiency expert Kerry Gleeson, who is the mastermind behind the Personal Efficiency Program, a unique foundation course developed in Sweden, aimed at improving levels of productivity, effectiveness, and efficiency at the workplace.

Since childhood, I have been a frequent explorer of many places. I have loved and enjoyed traveling. (Fortunately for me, my father worked in Singapore Airlines for over thirty years as a general manager and family members had travel entitlements). I am very grateful that at a very young age, I had the chance to be exposed to different cultures, people, and global events.

I learned that many people are not culturally intelligent and sensitive. It is a sad fact that universities are not giving proper attention to cultural diversity in today's education and learning. With today's global competitive space, the world is getting smaller and smaller every day with more interracial marriages and interracial working environments. Thus, we need to know how to work cohesively to attain success, effectiveness, and productivity. Without this, we become victims (instead of champions) of globalization. Everything is going global now with organizations being comprised of diverse nationalities. Being culturally intelligent can contribute great ease in communication flow and facilitating rapport, understanding, and teamwork. Managers must also know how to connect with their diverse subordinates. It's very important to leverage on diversity and make it your own competitive advantage!

Women today are juggling their time between work and personal life (home). Times have changed and so has the role of women, which has become more dynamic. Women are taking on greater responsibility now as compared to yesterday when women were left at home only to take care of domestic affairs. Advocacy of women in the workplace will uplift the value of womanhood, protect women's rights, gain more respect for women, and most importantly, will get career women to realize and maximize their potential. It's about building women's confidence and pride—teaching them how to walk tall in a male dominated society. It is evident that many women are doing male jobs now!

On the other hand, there are still societies that see women as second class citizens.

Wright

How essential is work-life balance in the pursuit of one's personal and professional success? And how relevant is it to individuals in the management of the successes they have achieved in their lives?

Angeline

Stop! Reflect now! Do you work to live? Or, do you live to work? The difference is the quality of living you will receive during this journey of your life.

Work-life balance plays two important roles in the pursuit of personal and professional success.

One, it ensures that the "technical" components of success are in the pink of health, including levels of productivity, efficiency, effectiveness. They are all a result of work-life balance, even the big bucks of commission and promotion you might get. Work-life balance is about good planning, right attitude toward deadlines, effective time management wherein you control time instead of battling with it, and most of all, it is about learning how to maneuver your life in your favor.

Second, it serves as the reason why homes are still intact and the people you love are still with you. It is the glue that binds the pieces of you—your family, friends, relatives, even your hobbies and favorite television shows.

There are successful people who have knowledge and skills but who have chosen to keep them rather than share them. There are those who are trying to be successful and who are sharing what they have acquired. There is a third group of people who are not successful but are always willing to learn and to overcome their shortcomings. If the first group of successful people does not manage successes effectively, they "fail to live" because they are not open to sharing their resources, knowledge, and skills with others who are in need. You gain success in living. More so, in today's economy, people must know how to manage success effectively and to live a purposeful life.

Wright

How would one know that he or she has achieved ultimate success in life?

Angeline

You are successful if you are healthy, happy, and have found your purpose in living.

Success is relative. Everyone measures ultimate success differently. Some claim that they have ultimate success when they have a billion dollars in their bank account. For some ladies, it'll be the time when their dream guy proposes marriage. For some families, it'll be the time when their children graduate from a university and are independent.

I would say that if you live to experience the different challenges that come with growing up, and you have the innate passion and desire to share your life's experiences with others so that they can improve theirs, then you've achieved and found the meaning of ultimate success.

When headhunted at the age of twenty-four to take on a sales position with British Airways, I was elated with the attractive remuneration package I received. I was feeling heaven. I was jumping for joy and sharing the happiness with my parents. It was a double promotion of sort. I was happy and I wanted to be successful.

It was against all odds because I joined the team being the youngest "alien" (someone who was headhunted from outside the company). It was a challenge within the organization because they had a culture then to promote internally. My existence had created emotions of insecurity for some who saw me as threat to their promotion opportunity.

I had a master's degree and I was young. I was determined to work hard to achieve recognition, and I was rewarded handsomely for my performance. I was successful. However, it was not ultimate success because I was not comfortable with my achievements. Strangely, I felt bad that I had done well, but my fellow colleagues were already starting to alienate me because of surpassing my sales targets every month, putting undue pressure on the others who were struggling to even meet them. It got more exciting when I was promoted to the head of that department! I knew I would be in for some pretty difficult times if I did not earn the respect from my team mates. I sought advice from my mother, who was a Customer Service Manager with Honeywell, Inc. then. She worked closely with a team of over thirty engineers, and I knew she could enlighten me. And she did. I felt more confident and I eventually succeeded to bond with my fellow colleagues to gain their support. I did achieve the feeling of ultimate success.

It is when you have fought the toughest battle, climbed the highest peak and swam the deepest waters that you feel you have won, and achieved ultimate success.

Wright

People have read about you and watched you in the media. Many people know that you are a successful speaker, coach, and entrepreneur. What do these people not know about you?

Angeline

I am who I am. Whichever angle you look at me, it is still me.

At five, I was a star in my little village. I won the coveted title of "Little Miss Beauty Queen." I did not know what that meant, I only knew that I received lots of attention and gifts from the crowd that Sunday afternoon when my mother dressed me up in a red *cheong sum*. The moment I took off the "crown" and dressed in my comfortable favorite "home-dress," I felt carefree and myself again—a five-year-old kid.

I guess each of us has an "outfit" for every occasion. We learn how to project a professional image in front of the audience, how to look glamorous in front of the cameras, and how to carry ourselves well in public to enhance our personal brand. These are all external factors. What's important is for people to know the internal being—the real person behind the outfits that cover the soul and the person in them.

People tend to forget that successful and famous celebrities are humans, too. They make mistakes and feel regretful about experiences in their lives. I have feelings and I have a soft spot. I cry! I am just the simple "girl next door." I enjoy the simplicity of eating local delicacies. I look forward to hanging out with my girlfriends from school and laugh at the weird hairstyles we had when we were young. I have always loved children. I adore them. I wear different hats in different occasions. I look prim and proper in the midst of media and that's one side. When you look at the other side, I am just a regular person playing different roles, wearing different outfits—a child, mother to children, wife, and friend to colleagues. We are humans too!

Wright

To be successful, what must be the primary focus, the journey or the destination?

Angeline

Living is a journey. Your purpose to live is the destination.

I recall that when I was young, I often felt so excited whenever I traveled to a new destination, be it on leisure or for business purposes. A few nights prior to the trip, I would get prepared and would read about the culture of the destination. I would pack sufficient clothing and food, ensuring that I would feel comfortable when I reached my destination. The anxiety built up the moment I arrived at the airport to depart.

Though I had many experiences and encounters over my forty years of traveling around the world, I am still excited and eager to know more, especially if I have to travel alone and have had no prior experiences at that destination. However, the anxiety soon turns to curiosity. Finally, I will look forward to every new adventure and every new experience during the journey.

Life: it can be assimilated to traveling to a new destination. Curious and excited, we look forward to taking on the journey and learning about the destination—firsthand. Similarly, we make preparations for the journey to make it thrilling and worthwhile. We plan on the fun activities that we can do so as to maximize the whole trip or journey. We even think about or sometimes appoint the people we want to share this journey with.

Sometimes we neglect the importance of planning and forget about its relevance to our lives. Work with a coach or a mentor and he or she will be able to share something about good and effective planning and what it can do to your life!

To enjoy every journey and to reach your destination successfully, incorporate the habit of:

- Planning ahead to add comfort to your trip;
- Preparing for contingencies;
- Praying earnestly for wisdom to make tough choices at crossroads;
- Having an open mind to embrace the changes;
- Staying positive when faced with challenges;
- Learning along the journey to accumulate your wealth in knowledge;
- Sharing and helping others to add meaningful stories in your journey;
- Experiencing the beauty of life.

Wright

If there is a standardized dictum among successful people, what would it be?

Angeline

I've been there, done that and I'm still learning how to do it better each day, every day of my life.

"We now accept the fact that learning is a lifelong process of keeping abreast of change. And the most pressing task is to teach people how to learn"—Peter F. Drucker.

"Give a man a fish and you feed him for a day. Teach him how to fish and you feed him for a lifetime"—Lao-tzu.

"It is necessary for us to learn from others' mistakes. You will not live long enough to make them all yourself"—Hyman G. Rickover.

"The highest result of education is tolerance"—Helen Keller.

"You will get all you want in life if you help enough other people get what they want"—Zig Ziglar.

"Success is the ability to go from one failure to another with no loss of enthusiasm"—Winston Churchill.

"Good, better, best. Never let it rest. Till your good is better and your better, best"—Motto of J. Furphy & Sons.

Reflecting on what had been said by all these successful people, we can see that they all touched on the key values of perseverance, learning, helping, positivity, and striving continuously.

Finally, remember to SPAM—my acronym to "Stay Positively Active and Motivated" to meet and overcome all of life's challenges.

About the Author

Angeline is the Founder and Principal Consultant of d'Oz International Pte Ltd, a professional learning and development solutions provider.

As a certified Coach and Master Trainer of PEP (Personal Efficiency Program), she has helped employees from various organizations to improve on their performance through proper management of time, duties and priorities at work. Throughout the years of personal and group coaching, she has gained a valuable knowledge and perspective of a person's life at the workplace.

Able to understand this, she upholds the importance of striking a balance between Work and Life. As a proficient speaker, she shares to her audience the practical practices to adopt when dipped into a busy and pressure-driven environment. She believes in SPAM (Stay Positively Active and Motivated) as the right formula to succeed in one's personal and professional life.

Another passion point of Angeline is communication, specifically in Cross-Cultural. As an inspiring trainer, she recognizes the importance of understanding diverse backgrounds. She believes that by having the right communication approach for every individual you meet or interact with, you are able to surpass the liabilities and troubles brought about by the unsettled natural differences.

She has acquired a wealth of experience in the international markets working with diverse cultures, and managed collaborations with Multi-Nationals, Ministries and Government Institutions in Singapore, Malaysia, Vietnam, Indonesia, China, Australia and the United Kingdom.

Angeline is a dynamic person with dynamic ways to engage people. She has helped many organizations and individuals at understanding the need to change, and individuals to move to a new dimension, opening new chapter in their lives. She has gained experience and exposure in the areas of organizational development and change management with major airlines such as Cathay Pacific, Qantas and British Airways.

She has twenty five years of experience in the areas of Management, Sales, Marketing, Distribution, E-Commerce, Training, Business, Consultancy and Coaching.

Angeline V Teo, Founder/Principal Consultant
d'Oz International Pte Ltd
7500A Beach Road, The Plaza #10-301,
Singapore 199591
Phone: (65) 6391 3733
www.d-oz.com
consultancy@d-oz.com

Chapter 8

Evelyn Johnson

David Wright (Wright)

Dr. Evelyn J. Johnson is founder of Rainbo Renaissance Creative Solutions, LLC. She has thirty-seven years' experience in the public schools of North Carolina and is a professional speaker with nearly four decades of leadership experience. Dr. Johnson understands the challenges facing educational communities in the twenty-first century. In addition to being a motivational speaker and leadership coach, Dr. Johnson is skilled and experienced in communication and employee motivation. She trains leaders how to release and empower the *untapped leadership potential* in their organizations. Her presentations are both entertaining and informative. She offers creative solutions to problem-solving and team development. She teaches that *people* make organizations great. She takes her clients out of their comfort zone and teaches them how to mix, match, and manage the generational challenges in the workplace.

Dr. Johnson, welcome to *Extreme Excellence*.

Evelyn Johnson (Johnson)

Thank you.

Wright

So what do you think of leadership; how does one become a person people will follow?

Johnson

Simply stated, leadership is the art of assembling the right people together toward a common goal. Sounds easy? Not so fast! A glimpse of America's past reveals that leadership was defined in the twentieth century by two words: "authority" and "power." The power was associated with the word "fear." During the '60s and '70s, school principals were the authority figures people looked up to, teachers ran their classrooms, ministers were respected figures, policemen were feared and obeyed, public officials were known for their integrity, and parents knew that the village looked out for every child. In retrospect, it was the time when we trusted and respected the people in their positions. It was also the time when the boss had control in the workplace, and no one questioned the decisions that were made.

As a Baby Boomer, I lived by one set of rules that were reinforced in the workplace. One might contend that those in charge led by force. To me, it was a sign of respect. I knew what was expected, and it was natural for me to conform.

As a successful classroom teacher, leading was all about my ability to influence my students to work together. Therefore, when I stepped into administration in 1983, I found adults reacted favorably to that same philosophy. In reality, I wasn't expected to have all of the answers. I shifted the paradigm when I asked one question: *What do you think?* Those four little words opened hearts and minds and gave birth to the word "empowerment." What they thought was important because I needed to build a team. As the leader, I was striving for excellence by creating an environment where success, fulfillment, and happiness were daily occurrences. John C. Maxwell, in his book *Be a People Person,* says the best way to become a person to whom others are drawn is to develop qualities that we are attracted to in others. He stated that we want others to:

1. Encourage us
2. Appreciate us
3. Forgive us
4. Listen to us
5. Understand us

What's it all about? It's about people interacting with others in a non-threatening environment where building relationships is the team's mission. A leader with those positive traits will attract followers. Isn't that what they want too? How team members behave toward each other is the test. A leader in this environment is humble, compassionate, and in tune with the needs of every person on the team.

Wright

Based on your background and experience, to what or to whom do you attribute your success as an effective leader?

Johnson

An effective leader never stops learning, therefore preparation is the key. My quest for excellence reveals my passion for building relationships and accomplishing goals through people. My greatest joy is watching people come together, share a dream, and focus on reaching their goals together. I learned early in my career that *what* I did as a leader was more important than *who* I was. As I worked with people in various settings, I found that leading people toward a common goal was my primary responsibility. In other words, it's not about the leader, it's about the actions one takes to achieve the stated goals.

To help you make a personal connection with me, let me tell you that I was born on a farm in eastern North Carolina. Many of my traits for leadership were developed watching my father make decisions on the farm. Farming is a risky business, and my dad always started with the end in mind. You know what you want, but there are no guarantees. One of the first lessons you learn is that there are so many variables that affect the harvest. A few of those variables include the soil, weather, timing, money, and most importantly, the workforce. Whether the crops were poor or plentiful, the only option was to do your best. My "leadingShip" traits— patience, humility, sticktoitiveness, disappointment, taking risk, decision-making, and my belief system—were life's lessons I learned from my daddy's farm. In 1969, I entered a second grade classroom with an elementary education degree and my farming skills toolbox, and both children and I reached our potential! I started by saying, "At the end of this year, we will be able to—" It worked, and every child achieved.

Wright

Over your thirty-seven years of experience in a leadership role, what would you say are the greatest challenges females have to overcome?

Johnson

The greatest difference I observed was in the salary scale. Women and men could have identical jobs, but men were paid more. The justification was that the man was the head of the household. Some even believed that women didn't work as hard as men. During the '60s and '70s, female administrators were often assigned to elementary schools in my district. Few would admit it, but men were considered better equipped to handle middle and high school age students.

I wanted to know why I didn't get a principalship at a middle school in the '80s, so I inquired. A Board of Education member said, *"You can't handle those big bucks."* I was fierce, but did a reality check when I applied for a high school, and again was denied the opportunity.

Gary N. Powell's comprehensive study, *Women and Men in Management,* made another observation: women tend to employ a more democratic, participative style while men take a more autocratic, directive approach. Throughout my thirty-seven years, I found that some women preferred to work for my male counterpart. Even though I am considered a nurturer, women often lamented that my expectations were too high. By no means am I suggesting that men don't nurture, it's just that I was expected to be more understanding, especially when deadlines or assignments weren't completed.

In her article, "Gendering Organizational Theory," Joan Acker argues that gender is part of the logic used in organizations to determine what practices will be adopted. Could this be a barrier that suggests women might shy away from jobs with long hours, business meetings, and events on weekends that provide for limited non-job related obligations?

That was then, and now, in the twenty-first century, women are competitive and salaries have improved. The role of the female has changed, and the day of the stay-at-home mom is almost extinct. Women have advanced up the leadership leader, but there continue to be inequities in salaries and some positions.

Wright

So how does an effective leader develop a winning team, and why do you say to do whatever it takes?

Johnson

In their book, *The One Minute Manager Builds High Performing Teams,* Kenneth Blanchard, Donald Carew, and Eunice Parisi-Carew list the following characteristics of a high performing team:

- Purpose
- Empowerment

- Relationships and communication
- Flexibility
- Optimal Performance
- Recognition and appreciation
- Morale

An effective leader must first determine if he or she has the right players on the team. A leader on a winning team has to provide a safe place where members play fair, take risks, keep improving, and most of all, care about each other. Members on the team are at their best when they know that each person is valued. Both authors addressed the need for the common thread of shared values for any organization to excel. The leader must be able to articulate what he or she sees as the mission of the team. The leader projects a snapshot of the end (vision) in his or her mind. When the workers catch the vision, in reality they'll do whatever is necessary to accomplish the goal.

Wright

What does the word "relationship" have to do with leadership and team development?

Johnson

Leadership is all about relationships! "Team" is defined as a group of people organized to work together. When people work together harmoniously, it is usually because they are working toward a common goal.

A successful leader knows how to tap into the strengths that each person brings to the organization. It is the leader's job to keep the team focused to accomplish the objectives. In other words, the leader drives the vision of the organization and empowers the team to complete the task.

To eliminate chaos, the team's roles and responsibilities are clearly defined. This opens the door to *trust*, the glue upon which effective relationships are built. The bottom line is assembling those persons who understand and respect each other. Without relationships, there is no team. The leader's job is that of an engineer, and must have a clear focus on the direction at all times.

Wright

Why is it important that an inspiring leader have a leadership coach?

Johnson

As I see it, coaching should never be an option for an aspiring leader. A coach can take an objective look from the inside out. This is important because we can't see ourselves as others do. A good coach observes the skill level of an individual on-site to identify areas that need improvement.

In the '60s, my first encounter with leadership was on-the-job training. People followed me because I wasn't afraid of change. I was charismatic, articulate, a natural leader, and they stated, *"so full of promise."* As an assistant principal, much of my professional development was based on the administration/supervision degree as well as what I thought that I needed.

My leadership journey began when I left a first grade classroom as a teacher and became a middle school assistant principal. I had no coach. Surely I could do this because I was an excellent teacher. That was partly right, but it's not quite that easy. Aspiring leaders need coaches who will take an active role in their professional development. A skill assessment inventory should be administered prior to entering into a "leadingShip" position. The coach's job is to use the inventory data to identify areas needing improvement.

Professional development training might include mentoring, goal-setting, and interfacing with other leaders, growing leaders, and removing obstacles. It's the coach who will challenge the aspiring leader to choose the area he or she wishes to improve. Desire alone does not make a good leader. It takes hard work and the willingness to see oneself through the eyes of an objective coach trained to guide one in *releasing the untapped potential to lead*. In summary, the coach's responsibility is to look (observe), do (prescribe), and say (feedback) what is necessary for the aspiring leader to strive for excellence.

Wright

Would you share with our readers what the driving force is to your passion for leadership?

Johnson

I love people; I am passionate about working with people and watching them grow. My leadership style allows me to build effective teams by empowering others. My style enables me to negotiate, mediate, facilitate, and communicate with little emphasis on power and control. It eliminates the need for hierarchy and results are achieved in a non-threatening manner.

When you are passionate about what you do, people gravitate to you. I call it "modeling your beliefs," and it can be contagious. Your passion sends the message: *Follow my lead*. When you are passionate about your job, you tend to be content and happy even where there are roadblocks. I am comfortable in my own skin and I am *real*. I believe I attract people to me because I am honest, sincere, approachable, credible, and set high expectations for myself and others.

Wright

What is the underlying message you want aspiring leaders to know about becoming a successful leader?

Johnson

Today's leader must understand what leadership is. It is not about who one is, it's what one does—*lead*. As the school principal, I learned the reality of leading—people don't want a boss who dictates, they want a leader who delegates. They want a leader who respects, understands, and empowers them to take risks without fear of reprisal. In my opinion, the greatest leaders are those who know how to serve others.

A great leader selects members on the team who are creative, problem-solvers, results-oriented, and who exhibit the potential to grow. A good leader knows how to follow and allows his or her team to evolve to the next level. In his book, *Good to Great*, Jim Collins says that the good to great leaders begin the transformation by getting the right people on the bus (and the wrong people off the bus) and then figure out where to drive it. The key point is not just the idea of getting the right people on the team. The key point is the "who" questions come before the "what" decisions— before vision, before strategy, before organization, structure, before tactics . . .

In other words, the leader's success depends upon being prepared to lead, so that hiring the right people is not a problem.

Wright

As the leader, how do you encourage others to discover their untapped leadership potential in team development?

Johnson

In my schools, I served as an example and my strength to get results through people made all the difference. The best way for anyone to learn is by doing. The workplace where creativity is encouraged promotes professional growth.

Discovering potential in others requires discussions, observations, interactions, and reflections in varied settings.

My job as leader is to tap into the strengths of every member on the team and develop a plan for growth. Defining roles and responsibilities allows team members to experience a high level of success. The leader's job is to trust and believe by encouraging every member to do his or her part. I found that the confidence level of every member goes up when he or she is valued. When people do what they are good at, they simply get better at it. The leader who encourages taking risks without reprisal provides a safe place to grow leadership. The *untapped potential* to lead will surface under these conditions.

As a leadership coach, I encourage leaders to make professional development a priority for every member on the team. It's the best way to grow leaders for the future. In summary, one must be honest, sincere, and *real* to discover the *untapped potential* nestled deep within others. A great leader makes training a priority by allocating adequate resources and time.

Wright

Why do you say that an effective leader is one who knows how to serve others?

Johnson

In my opinion, you can't lead if you don't know how to follow. One can serve others more effectively when he or she is able to step out of the leadership role into that of the follower. The role reversal provides opportunities to observe potential leadership. Great leaders know how to delegate the leader's role with a high level of confidence. Another way to express this idea is to empower others to share the role so that potential leaders will emerge.

Wright

What did you mean when you coined the phrase, "you are who you are based on where you come from, when it's your choice to move or stand still"?

Johnson

It's true: *You are who you are based on where you come from when it's your choice to move or stand still.* We have choices in life, and it is up to us to remain where we start or to take it to the next level.

I'm number four of six siblings, and some believed I would never leave the farm. I was a dreamer, and farm work during the hot summer months was not in my definition of the future. I had no control over the sun, it was fulfilling its purpose, but making a living on the farm was certainly not my purpose. I knew I couldn't change where I started, but I could definitely change my future. Only God knows my destiny, but He gave me knowledge and the ability to take it to the next level. Care to guess my next level? I graduated from high school and the rest is history.

Growing up, I quickly realized that remaining on the farm was not an option. Leaving allowed me to follow my dream and the next level was in the schoolhouse. To advance to the next level, I stepped out of my comfort zone to chase a career of helping others realize their dreams. For thirty-seven years my comfort zone has been outside of the box. I am happy with my choices, and I continue to strive for excellence—my ultimate goal. Why do I say you are who you are based on where you come from when it's your choice to move or stand still? That's just the way life is.

I had no choice in choosing my family, but I controlled my future. Being the product of a sixth grade walk-out (my father) and my mother who was an eleventh grade drop-out, I knew that I would determine my destiny.

Wright

Would you elaborate for our readers what your "eleventh commandment for people who work with people" is?

Johnson

During my thirty-seven years in public education, I met many people who didn't seem to have the passion for working with others. Their motive for leadership had more to do with status, monetary gain, being in the good old boy or girl network, and/or "it's my time to move up the ladder." It appeared that their hearts were not in their work, and their followers always knew it. Their priority tended to be satisfying the boss.

I believe that we do our best when we are fulfilling our needs while working with others. Each leader brings a set of values from his or her background and experience that affects the choices he or she makes. It is my job to strive to do my best. I've learned that what I believe about others is a reflection of who I am.

If excellence is striving to do our best, a leader must embrace lifelong learning. Leading is my calling, so each day I seek to get better at growing people. I became an extraordinary leader because I knew what I wanted and understood how to fulfill my dreams. I am truly committed in my career, and no matter what happens, I know that the best is yet to come! Pearl Buck said, *The secret of joy in work is contained in one word: "excellence." To know how to do something well is the joy of it.*

The Eleventh Commandment is simply a mandate to leaders: *If you don't love working with people, get out of the business!* You must love what you do to get better at it. Fake people need not enter the field of true leadership!

Wright

Well, what an interesting conversation. You've given me a lot of things to think about here today, and I've enjoyed it immensely; this has been very informative for me. I really appreciate all the time you've taken to answer these questions and all the valuable information you've shared here.

Today we've been talking with Dr. Evelyn J. Johnson. She is the Founder of Rainbo Renaissance Creative Solutions. She trains and empowers people to release untapped leadership potential to strengthen organizations and I think we have found here today that she knows what she's talking about—at least I'm going to listen to her.

Dr. Johnson, thank you so much for being with us today on *Extreme Excellence.*

Johnson

It was my pleasure.

About the Author

Dr. Evelyn J. Johnson is founder of Rainbo Renaissance Creative Solutions, LLC. She draws from her thirty-seven years' experience in public schools of North Carolina. She is a professional speaker with nearly four decades of leadership experience who understands the challenges facing educational communities in the twenty-first century. In addition to being a motivational speaker and leadership coach, Dr. Johnson is skilled and experienced in communication and employee motivation. She trains leaders how to release and empower the *untapped leadingShip potential* in their organizations. Her presentations are both entertaining and informative. She offers creative solutions to problem-solving and team development. She teaches that *people* make organizations great. She warns aspiring leaders in the twenty-first century that "leadingShip is in and boss-ship is out." She takes her clients out of their comfort zone when she teaches them how to mix, match, and manage the generational challenges in the workplace.

Dr. Johnson's humble beginnings in a rural North Carolina farmhouse took her to the top of her game in education in the schoolhouse. Her most requested keynotes are: *The Eleventh Commandment for People Who Work With People, 5 Hot Tips to Supercharge Your LeadingShip,* and *Mixing, Matching, and Managing Four Generations in the Workplace.*

She presents seminars, keynotes, and workshops that enlighten, entertain, and educate while providing participants with empowering tools they can use immediately. All services can be customized to meet her clients' needs.

Dr. Evelyn J. Johnson
309 NC 111–122 S.
Tarboro, NC 27886
252.823.4898
evelyn.j.johnson@gmail.com
www.empoweringdoctor.com

Chapter 9

Barbie Reed

THE INTERVIEW

David Wright (Wright)

Today we're talking with Barbie K. Reed. Barbie's background as an entrepreneur, national trainer, professional speaker, workshop facilitator, staff development consultant, life coach, and communication expert for the past thirty years brings a wide range of experience and expertise. A multi-dimensional speaker, Barbie addresses many issues including enhancing cultural sensitivity, diversity training, customer service, developing positive attitudes, team-building, leadership, management training, self-esteem, and personal development along with helping others to reach their fullest potential.

She is also highly sought after for her expertise as an educational consultant with administrators, teachers, parents, and especially for her transformational work with young people. She is internationally recognized as a communication expert for her dynamic work with all kinds of organizations in helping them to enhance their communication skills, resolve conflict more effectively, improve team communication with coworkers, and interact with customers to give the best quality services. She does this with a powerful program called Psycho Geometrics®, in which she is the first African American licensed consultant.

Created by Dr. Susan Dellinger, Psycho Geometrics is an international program that has been used for more than thirty years by more than one million people in twenty-four countries, from the Fortune 500 companies to schools to governmental agencies to healthcare organizations to not-for profit-groups, and many other businesses and community groups. Barbie is a highly energetic presenter and her clients describe her as powerful, motivating, captivating, inspiring, and passionate. Her keynotes and workshops are customized for all types of groups. Her workshops with employees have garnered rave reviews. Barbie is also available to facilitate all-day retreats for management staff.

Barbie, welcome to *Extreme Excellence.*

Barbie Reed (Reed)

Thank you, David. I'm so excited about this wonderful project.

Wright

Why should cultural sensitivity be addressed in the work environment?

Reed

David, for the first time in history there are four generations in the workplace; can you believe that? Each generation defines work ethics in a different way and has its own sets of values. Each responds to different forms of motivation, and each interprets the way things are done differently. But let me tell you about the four generations.

The Veterans are also known as the Silent Generation or Mature Generation. They were born somewhere between 1922 and 1943, and there are about 52 million of them. Then there are the Baby Boomers. That's where I am. Members of the Baby Boomer Generation were born somewhere between 1943 and 1960; there are about 73.2 million of them. Then there are the Generation X'ers; that's the generation my son belongs to. They were born somewhere between 1960 and 1980; there are probably about 70.1 million of them. Next we have the Generation Y'ers (also known as Millennials). They were born somewhere between 1980 and 2000, and today there are about 69.7 million of them.

As I was telling you, each generation brings different dynamics to the work environment, which causes some challenges for managers and leaders. I would love to share with you some of the different aspects of these generations and how they affect the work environment because I really think managers and supervisors who are working with these groups would benefit from this valuable information.

Members of the Silent Generation believe that hard work and dedication leads to rewards. You'll find them coming to work on time, they rarely miss work, they're committed to the organization, and they respect authority.

Then there are the Boomers—they've been called the "Me Generation." They're competitive, hard-working, and they're the generation that started the sixty-hour work week. They get the job done at any cost, are seen as sacrificing personal life to achieve professional goals, and today they have a new outlook about getting a life.

Generation X'ers are considered to be "the latchkey kids." They digest information rapidly, they have witnessed corporate downsizing, and they might not sacrifice personal life for a company, so they're a little bit different than the other generations—the Boomers and the Silent Generation.

Then we have the Generation Y'ers or Millennials. They're cooperative, civic minded, and intellectually curious. They have mostly known affluence. They want meaningful work that makes a difference in the world and they value information and technology.

Now here's the key thing: in order to eliminate generation discord, it's important to understand what makes each generation tick, what their core values are, what they expect of their leaders, how they define success, and how they are different from you.

But the whole goal, and the reason why I truly believe that it's important to address cultural sensitivity in the workplace today, is that we have to see the importance of respecting each other, understanding each group's values, recognizing those differences and not seeing them as a negative. By doing this we'll be able to communicate and have patience with each other, we'll be able to appreciate what each of us brings to the team, and the perspective that each generational group has.

So with the four generations coming together there is a need of cultural sensitivity, which is more important than people realize. Years ago my training was more about racial diversity; however, generational diversity is becoming a bigger diversity issue because of the cultural background that each generation brings to the work environment. I've been doing a lot of workshops involving these generational groups and it's been really a lot of fun; I'm excited to be a part of this new movement and this new kind of training. I'm finding that organizations are absolutely loving this training. They are discovering that it's creating a new-found communication within their organization and eliminating many potential problems.

Wright

So why is it important to you to help people reach their fullest potential?

Reed

It's really important to me because many years ago I once heard a quote that was mind-blowing to me. I don't have any idea where it came from, but it stuck with me all these years. It stated that "90 percent of people die having realized only 10 percent of their potential." What this says to me is that many people never ever even experience it in their lifetime.

When I heard that I decided to do some research on it. I began to look at what it means to live your fullest potential. One of the things that I found out is that many people lack motivation. In some cases, people sabotage their own success because deep down they don't feel that they can be successful. In some cases they have not seen a lot of people in their families or community be successful.

Personally, for me, I'm a risk-taker and when I begin a project or idea, I don't focus on the failure aspect. I don't even really talk about the idea with many people because their negativity or lack of vision could deter me away from taking the risk. There are times when we sabotage ourselves by worrying about what other people think of us. A family member, a coworker, or a friend passes judgment on our dream, and all of a sudden that's enough to stop us from moving forward.

I want to share a story that I use in my workshops that I think sets the stage for what I'm talking about; it's called "The Man Who Lived by the Side of the Road." He had no radio, he had trouble with his eyes, so he had no newspaper, but he sold good hot dogs. He put up a sign on the highway telling how good the hot dogs he was selling were. He stood by the side of the road and called out, "Buy a hot dog mister!" And the people bought. He increased his meat and bun orders and he built a bigger stand to take care of his trade.

When his son came home from college to help him, something happened. His son said. "Father, haven't you been listening to the radio? Business is terrible. The international situation is terrible, and the domestic situation is even worse." Whereupon his father thought, "Well, my son has been to college. He listens to the radio and reads the paper, and he ought to know."

So the father cut down his bun order, took down his advertising signs, and no longer bothered to stand on the highway to sell hot dogs. His hot dogs sales fell almost overnight.

"You were right son," said the father. "Business is really terrible." The author of this story is unknown, but can you imagine—the man allowed someone else to deter his dream.

I would like to share with you ten characteristics that I believe people must have in order to realize their fullest potential:

1. They have to have a dream.

2. They have to have ambition along with passion.
3. They must be strongly motivated toward achievement.
4. They must be focused individuals.
5. They take responsibility for their actions.
6. They look for solutions to problems.
7. They work with and cooperate well with other people.
8. They are enthusiastic people.
9. They are optimistic people who look for the bright side of things.
10. They are life-long learners, always seeking to improve themselves, and enhancing their skills and talents.

Wright

So as a communication expert, what program have you found beneficial in your staff development training?

Reed

One of the trainings that I get rave reviews about is an international program called Psycho Geometrics in which I am a Licensed Consultant. As you mentioned in the beginning, it is being used in twenty-four countries, and with over one million people. Dr. Susan Dellinger, founder and creator of Psycho Geometrics, reveals that there are five dominant behavior types. Each one of these types has very distinct and predictable patterns of observable behavior. Once you understand these patterns you have the key to unlocking your ability to get along with nearly anyone. By understanding your own communication style you'll be able to leverage your strength and avoid your weaknesses. Now there are five geometric shapes to consider:

1. Boxes are hard workers. Dependable, reliable people, they love routine and give attention to details.
2. Triangles are leaders. They are the movers and the shakers of the world. They are bottom line people and natural risk-takers.
3. Rectangles are flexible and open to change and new ideas. They're people who are in transition.
4. Circles are highly sociable, very verbal, and are great communicators and listeners. They work well with others and are very caring people.
5. Squiggles are highly creative people. They're your ideal people—innovative, interested in concepts and theory, and spontaneous. They become bored quickly.

I met Dr. Dellinger probably about thirty-two years ago while attending a training sponsored by Career Track in my hometown. Never did I imagine in my lifetime, that thirty-some years later I would meet this outstanding woman again. I actually met her on three occasions.

The third time, I decided to go on her Web site to see what Dr. Dellinger was doing with Psycho Geometrics. You see, I had been utilizing her communication system for all of these years, personally and professionally, with my marketing skills, in my networking, with my own company, with my customers/clients, and in my interactions with others. I found this program to be phenomenal in helping to change the way I communicated with people on a day-to-day basis. At this point I decided I wanted to know more about it in helping others.

After completing a survey on her Web site she called me and learned that I was a national training consultant. She decided to give me an opportunity to do an audition video. I am thrilled to say that my video was accepted, and I was on my way to being a part of this powerful international program that is changing the way people communicate with others. I'm just having a great time helping organizations and businesses to utilize this innovative system.

In talking with Dr. Dellinger, I learned that there are a lot of programs out there—Myers Briggs, True Colors, and DISC—to name a few. Dr. Dellinger says her system is unique because, "It is simpler to administer, you only have five shapes, as opposed to sixteen personalities variants in the MBTI. It is easily remembered (visual shapes are not dependent on word meanings on a written test). It is quickly understood (shapes/symbols carry universal meanings). Once you know the meanings, you have it as a part of you. It is also based on solid, psychological research by Dr. Carl Jung." I'm appreciating the opportunity to be a part of a great group of consultants from around the world who are also presenting this powerful communication system.

Wright

Can people's attitudes about their jobs affect the way they interact with their clients and their customers?

Reed

Most definitely! I once heard that 80 percent of working people are not happy with what they are doing—that's four out of five people—so it is very important for people to change the way they view their work. Let's face it, most people do not receive as much satisfaction from their jobs as they could if they had a more positive attitude toward what they're doing, saw the bigger picture of who they are helping, and what their product or service is doing to help improve the community.

The question we need to ask is what can be done about it? Instead of viewing work as something to be endured, we need to view it as a primary source of satisfaction and happiness and strive to make it happen. This means digging deeply within ourselves and changing our focus on the work that we do. For some people that is hard. Think about it this way: 80 percent of your life is spent working, so if you don't take a look at how you feel about your job, it's going to affect other people around you, your interaction with your coworkers, your customers, and your supervisors. By engaging in apathetic behavior, by doing the absolute minimum required, you only train yourself to be blind and unresponsive to opportunity when it does finally arise, and then you have developed a reputation of being a slacker or a person with a negative attitude, which could precede you in the future.

I provide a workshop program called, "Take this Job and Love It," and one of the things that I look at when I provide this training is your relationship of how you feel about your job and your relationship of how you feel about yourself. I will give you some tools to get unstuck and deal with your job more positively.

Many times people get stuck in a negative attitude, blaming it on the boss/supervisor and blaming it on everybody else. They fail to realize that in order to create excellence in their life they need to maintain a standard of excellence, no matter what the outward circumstances are around them—this is the best strategy. It is best for *you* because you retain power over your own life and give yourself the most resourceful options.

If your reputation is that of maintaining a standard of excellence and growing your personal skills, then you will have more opportunity of being elevated. You might make it even easier to find a better situation elsewhere and your profile won't be seen as negative and bitter. People sometimes spend their lifetime trying to find the best job, and the job might not be the situation, it might just be taking the simple step of changing their attitude about how they see their jobs and the choices that they've made through the years about the kind of future they wanted in the work world.

Wright

Should individuals in leadership positions consider how they motivate their staff?

Reed

Yes, as a manager or supervisor, your impact on employee motivation is immeasurable. Your words, your body language, and the expression on your face as a leader can impact the way you motivate your staff. Remember, you are providing an environment, climate, or atmosphere either for positive motivation or not. Many managers are not seeing the importance of this and they feel it is not their responsibility to motivate their staff. They should realize that they can make or break a day. If they come to work feeling motivated, it affects their interaction with their employees.

There's an exercise I use in my management workshops that I have found so important. I ask leaders to think of one person, preferably someone who is difficult for them to deal with and who reports directly to them. I ask them to look at five things about this individual:

1. What do I know about this person's professional goals?
2. What does this person enjoy most about his or her job?
3. What does this person enjoy least about his or her job?
4. What three things does this person seem excited about when talking about personal time?
5. What kind of task does this person volunteer to do and with what result?

It's very interesting when I have department heads, supervisors, and managers do this assessment. Very few of them are able to answer these questions because the majority of them haven't taken the time to know the people they supervise. You can't really motivate or empower someone if you don't even know that person or the person's aspirations. And most of all, if you don't communicate with your employees with honor and respect, it's going to get in the way of motivating them. One of my favorite quotes about this thought is by Sam Walton: "Outstanding leaders go out of their way to boost the self-esteem of their personnel. If people believe in themselves, it's amazing what they can accomplish."

Wright

Can people's lack of passion affect how they go about their day-to-day life?

116

Reed

Wow, my favorite subject. The quote and the passage I use in my workshops describe passion: "Passion: is the Energy that Comes From Bringing More of You Into What You Do." Here's the point: if you lack passion in your life, it will be difficult to feel energized in every relationship in your life, including your interaction with your customers, your coworkers, and your family also. Imagine a career where you feel energized by and engaged in your work. You look forward to work in the morning even if it's a Monday, you feel great about how you spend your day, you have the energy at the end of your workday to spend the rest of your life fully, you get excited when you tell people about what you do for a living, and you believe deeply in the work that you do.

The point I'm making, David, is that discovering our passion and purpose is vital to our joy, our wellbeing, our mental attitude, and our enthusiasm for life.

I have chosen an acronym for the word PASSION that I use personally for me. It motivates me:

The P stands for Purpose. Knowing what you want and doing it because it expresses who you really are. When I think of Oprah Winfrey, Mother Teresa (when she was alive), Sam Walton (when he was alive), and Bill Gates I realize they're there on purpose, they've lived the life they were born to live. It would be hard for them to imagine doing anything else. They don't need goals to motivate them, they do it anyway—they have *passion*.

The A stands for Attitude. Attitude is the way you see things mentally and the mood you transmit to others. Nothing contributes to life more than a positive attitude. Working with a person with a positive attitude is a delightful experience.

The S stands for Success. Success is not something you achieve or something you attain, such as education or money, a house, a nice car, a family, but it is something that you live. The question to ask is: can you live success? I believe you can. I hope you live success each and every day you get up and I hope you share it with those you interact with each and every day.

The S stands for Self-starter. A self-starter is an energetic person with unusual initiative. Self-starters are willing to go after what they want with a fervor that says they can accomplish those goals and dreams they want to attain.

The I stands for Inspiration. What inspires you to get up in the morning and do what you do each and every day? In our lifetime we meet many types of people. The ones who stand out for me are the ones who overcome challenges and have a positive outlook on life in spite of those challenges. We all face challenges in our life, but how we handle those challenges and how we look at life is what truly matters.

There are three things to keep in mind: we can focus on the good and move forward, we can focus on the negative and wallow in self pity, or we can take the negative situation, whatever it may have been, and use it as inspiration to move our lives forward positively and use it for the foundation of our passion.

The O stands for Optimism. Optimism is about whether you see the glass half full or half empty. On those days when nothing in your life seems to be going right, it could be really tough to see the silver lining among all those clouds. However, during these times it's important to see the good in even the worst situation. An optimistic attitude benefits not only your mental health, but can also be the pathway for the goals and dreams you want to accomplish.

And the last but not least is Navigating. Navigating your life is about realizing what is it that you're passionate about and making a commitment to remove the barriers that get in the way of your living your fullest potential. I did not get around to doing this until I was forty. First of all I was afraid of being successful, second I was stuck in some unhealed childhood issues, and third, I was busy sabotaging my own success, which got in the way of my fulfilling my goals and dreams. Even now into my mid fifties, I am still on the journey to turning this all around so as to live a more passionate life.

Wright

Why should employees be able to relate to their mission statement of their company or their organization?

Reed

When you go into many companies and many organizations, businesses, schools, and different groups, they all have a mission statement probably displayed somewhere. Often employees pay no attention to it or don't even know it, from what I have found over the years. The greatest small business tries to get its employees to actually buy into that mission statement and believe in it. When employees don't understand what the business is about or they are forced to heed some statement that they are asked to buy into and believe, it can affect morale and morale will begin to suffer.

I remember several years ago providing some training with an organization (it was a healthcare organization, I believe). The organization had received negative evaluation reports by the state several times. The leaders asked my company to come in and do a customer service training, which we did, but it didn't go as well as I would have liked. The response was good and they listened but it didn't change the evaluations they were receiving. So then we came back and did diversity training, and still the negative evaluations kept coming from the state. They could not figure out what the problem was.

Finally I asked, "How long ago was your mission statement written?" Come to find out the mission statement had been written some forty years ago, and currently they had no buy-in from anyone who worked there. So I suggested we do a training to recreate the mission statement and let employees be a part of it. They then began to see improvements needed for their organization. The statement wasn't some long fifty-word document, but it was something people were able to buy into and feel they were a part of.

After checking back months later they began to see a difference in the service that they gave, response back from the state was better, and it also affected their interactions with each other.

From that experience I would say that an organization's mission statement is a key component in motivating its staff.

Wright

What are some tips that you can share to help build powerful teams?

Reed

There are seven that I have been using:

1. *Build high self-esteem in yourself and others.* I believe that self-esteem is the main ingredient for successful personal and interpersonal relationships.
2. *Be an effective communicator.* The key to effective communication is not only speaking with clarity, but also listening with undivided attention. Remember, listening is more than listening with the ears—it's listening with your eyes and also listening with your heart.
3. *Remember that everyone has unique strengths and talents that they bring to the team.* It is important to use these strengths

for a common goal and to determine what is in the best interest of servicing your customers.

4. *Respect others on the team.* Develop personal respect for the individuals and professional respect for the roles and responsibilities they have on the team.

5. *Deal with conflict positively.* The way we handle conflict will determine whether it is constructive or destructive.

6. *Be enthusiastic.* Your enthusiasm is the key to motivating yourself and others on your team.

7. *Understand your team members.* You must understand the personality of your team members. By understanding the Psycho Geometrics Shapes of your coworkers, you can communicate with each other more effectively.

As we discussed earlier about these five personalities created by Dr. Susan Dellinger, there are pluses and minuses to all the shapes. No single one of them is the most desirable, neither is any person only one shape—most likely you'll find aspects of your coworkers' personalities in all five shapes, but one will dominate. Each individual on your team has a dominate shape, and even your team has a shape. Understanding this will help create better communication within your team, other departments, and the primary organization as a whole.

One of my favorite quotes is by Henry Ford about teamwork: "Coming together is a beginning, keeping together is progress, and working together is success."

Wright

So whose job is it to build the morale of the organization?

Reed

Many people think that it is the job of the supervisor/manager. Honestly, however, I think it's the job of both the supervisor/manager and the individual people themselves to build the morale of the organization. But it's the supervisor/manager and other leaders who are in charge and who keep morale moving forward. A favorite quote I use in my leadership training is, "You can't buy your employees' enthusiasm, hearts, minds, and souls—you must earn these."

A sign of morale problems is easy to describe as a state of mind, a mood, or a mental condition. When I've gone into organizations and I've seen the morale dying, often there is a lack of motivation. In some cases it may include a problem with the manager/supervisor. If managers/supervisors are not motivated, they don't like their job, and they fall into that 80 percent of working people who are not happy with what they are doing, then the people under them will be not motivated. It's important for leaders to come out from behind their desks, talk to employees, and constantly interact with their staff—include contact with *all* team members, not just a few. It's also important for leaders to stay alert about what's going on with staff and keep communication open.

It's key for them to keep morale up by praising them more than they criticize. When they do that it can make a difference in their interaction with each other. They want to urge team members to keep trying when they fail and help them improve their performance.

Start new employees off with a challenging task, but make sure they have a reasonable chance to succeed. Encourage poor performers instead of harping on what they've done wrong so they don't become frustrated and lose confidence in themselves and the teamwork process.

The bottom line, I think, in keeping the morale going is to create a winning atmosphere. Let team members take a part in decision-making as much as you can because most workers cherish the opportunity to give input on decisions that affect their jobs. By doing this you help to empower them and you motivate them.

Another thing is learning to respect them as human beings, which is a valuable part to teamwork. I feel that this is a major part in helping to build morale. I think it's also up to the staff to know that they can affect the morale too and they should seek to have the same respect for their supervisor; but it's something that they must earn.

Wright

So what do employees want in a job?

Reed

According to research I've read, today's employees are looking for more than just a paycheck; that was the belief in the past. Sometimes they're willing to earn less if it means a situation with greater job satisfaction and more fulfilling work. Some researchers found also that employees want flexible hours to balance family responsibilities.

After more than thirty years of training some of the things that I've heard that employees want include:

1. *Job security.* They want to feel that they can wake up in the morning and still have a job.
2. *A sympathetic manager or supervisor.* They want someone who can give help or suggestions with their personal problems or even care about what's happening with them.
3. *Interesting work.* They also want appreciation for what they do.
4. *To be kept informed.* They want to feel like they're included in the loop in what's happening in the company.
5. *To be listened to and respected.* They want to know that their ideas and thoughts have value.
6. *Good working conditions.* They also want loyalty from their coworkers.
7. *Tactful discipline.* They want thoughtful discipline from a manager or supervisor who has earned their respect.
8. *Opportunities.* They want to grow in their job and have opportunities for increased skills development.
9. *To be challenged.* They want to see the end result of their work.
10. *Contribution.* They want to feel that they are a valuable part of the big picture of the organization.

Wright

Why should individuals see the importance of getting along with their boss, no matter how they feel about them?

Reed

I believe that if you develop a good relationship with your boss, it can enhance communication and make it easier. A good working relationship with your boss—the person you report to—can make you want to go to work. Your boss may be the second most important person in your career—second only to yourself. It's a special relationship, one that can be rewarding or painful. There are certain aspects about your boss that you may not like, but if you create a good supervisor/employee relationship, it is achievable—I truly believe that. You must realize that your boss is human, just like you are. Your boss has bad days and makes mistakes too. Your boss brings value to the organization and to you, even if he or she only determines your next pay increase or whether or not you are approved for a promotion.

Keep in mind too that your boss also has a boss he or she has to answer to. There are several things you want to keep in mind: pay attention to his or her style and how does your boss like to be updated? Does he or she prefer e-mails, voice-mails, drop-in visits? When you know this it will enhance a good relationship and it will build trust and confidence with your boss. Seek to enhance communication with your boss—get the inside scoop on who he or she is.

What it boils down to more than anything else is how well you and your boss can deal with the emotional rollercoaster of everyday life, and perhaps most important, how each of you view your job. Getting along with your boss, or other people, for that matter, includes understanding and reacting to their personality traits—get inside your boss's head.

A few years back I created a workshop using a personality program that will help with getting along with your boss. Once an employee understands the personality of the boss, and the boss understands the personality of the employee, it can enhance communication between them. Then each will have the skills to interact effectively. They will know what they like, what they don't like—mutual understanding will build a better relationship.

A better relationship between employees and their bosses results in better service for customers and creates a more positive work environment for all.

Wright

So what are some of the programs that you have received rave reviews for?

Reed

I do a lot of training on communication issues, customer service, leadership, cultural sensitivity, supervisory training, diversity, youth empowerment, and many other personal and professional development topics. There are several that I want to highlight.

The first one is called "Understanding People and the Art of Communicating with Them." This is an entertaining, enlightening, and thoroughly enjoyable interpersonal communication training that has been drawing rave reviews from individuals and organizations across the country. I have presented it to transportation groups, government organizations, health departments, nursing homes, hospitals, schools, educators, colleges, child welfare groups, businesses, not-for-profit groups, insurance professionals, the automotive sales industry, religious organizations, and many other groups. I utilize the international Psycho Geometrics system in this training program. It's helping people to know how to work together as a team. It's fun and incorporates a hands-on approach, and it's down to earth. People walk away knowing what their communication style is, what shapes push their buttons, and skills to deal with them. The program will enhance their communication with their team members and help to handle conflict more effectively. It's a unique and innovative program that is outstanding.

Another one is called "Enhancing Cultural Sensitivity in the Workplace." In today's multi-generational environment, a lack of cultural sensitivity can generate serious ramifications for an organization. To enhance organizations' chances for success, employees must be given the skills to interact with others with the utmost respect. This training includes examining the different generations in the workplace. It's an uplifting and inspiring presentation that challenges audiences to examine their personal biases and behaviors in order to enhance their understanding of others and be more effective with others from a different generational group.

Another one is called, "Take This Job and Love It." People enjoy this one because they come in with a preconceived mindset from the title of the workshop. This is a highly interactive workshop that has been designed to enhance employees' present interpersonal skills and at the same time help them to become more resilient when dealing with the public. They receive insights and strategies that will help them on a personal and professional level.

Another presentation I enjoy providing is titled "I've Got a New Attitude." This is a high-energy presentation that involves people taking a look at their attitudes about life and themselves. It will give them some tools and skills to develop a new attitude.

Another one that I feel very strongly about is called "Building Resilient Youth for the Twenty-first Century." This highly interactive and profound presentation is designed to help participants develop high expectations for all youth as they empower them to reach their fullest potential. Participants will be given unique strategies that will motivate youth into positive actions. It demonstrates the importance of never giving up on a child no matter what his or her background may have been. This is one workshop that has been getting rave reviews with educators, parents, and many conference participants.

Wright

Well, what a great conversation. I really appreciate the time you've spent with me here this morning answering all of these questions. I have really learned a lot and I've taken a ton of notes about the different characteristics of all four work forces. I've written down ten methods of success, starting with having a dream and ambition, right down to the last one, which I think is very important—being a life-long learners. I think you've got a great thing going here with your training programs. I want you to know that I appreciate your spending the time here to explain them.

Reed

I'm excited about this opportunity and I look forward to continuing to use my life to make a difference in the world.

Wright

Today we've been talking with Barbie K. Reed. She is an internationally recognized communication expert for her dynamic work with all kinds of organizations, helping them to enhance their communication skills, to resolve conflict more effectively, improve team communication, interact with customers, and give the best quality services. She does this with a powerful program called Psycho Geometrics.

Barbie, thank you so much for being with us today on *Extreme Excellence.*

Reed

Thank you, David.

About the Author

Barbie K. Reed is a dynamic and passionate speaker, a much in-demand consultant, as well as a highly sought-after trainer and workshop facilitator who blends content-rich presentations with an entertaining and motivating style that inspires people to positive action. People walk away from her training programs receiving a double benefit that they didn't expect—that of enjoying themselves while learning practical, immediately applicable skills that can impact them personally and professionally.

She has a wonderful ability to inform and inspire audiences toward developing a more enthusiastic attitude about their jobs and life as a whole. She is the CEO of B.K.R. Unlimited, a national training consultant company that focuses on helping people to discover their unlimited potential and Nurturing Yourself Seminars, an organization that works to help empower women and girls to transform their lives to new levels. She is an up and coming author and community leader who believes in reaching back to help others revolutionize their lives into better situations for themselves.

She is also an internationally recognized communication expert and Licensed Psycho Geometrics® consultant who helps workshop participants discover more about themselves, their attitudes, and the people with whom they come in contact daily. With this dynamic communication system that is being used by over one million people and in twenty-four countries, people are being shown the most effective techniques to improve seemingly incompatible relationships and enhance communication with clients/customers, coworkers, supervisors/managers, and their family members.

She resides in Florida with her family, but is available to come *wherever* you are if you are looking for a trainer, *staff development* consultant, workshop/retreat facilitator, keynote speaker or conference presenter who has a powerful inspirational message that is delivered in a passionate way leaving your employees, management staff, workshop/retreat participants, and conference attendees wanting more.

She was recently honored with a "Woman of Distinction" award in the business category. This award was presented to her by Joan Rivers who was a speaker at the GALA.

Barbie K. Reed
P.O. BOX 1542
Daytona Beach, FL 32115-1542
Office: 386 255-0020
Fax: 386 238 0045
barbiekreed@bellsouth.net
www.bkrunlimited.com
www.nurturingseminarsforyou.com

Chapter 10

Cindy Solomon

THE INTERVIEW

David Wright (Wright)

Today we're talking with Cindy Solomon. Cindy Solomon is founder and CEO of Solomon and Associates Inc., an organization passionately committed to helping organizations build long-term and profitable relationships with their customers, their leaders, and their employees. As one of the most sought-after leadership, customer service strategic consultants, and keynote presenters in the country, Cindy brings her provocative and innovative insights to literally thousands of leaders and hundreds of organizations each year. Her client list includes a who's who of national and international industry associations and some of the largest gatherings of executives in the country with clients such as Eli Lilly and Company, Oracle, Cisco, Telluride Ski & Golf Company, Genentech, The Association of Nurse Practitioners, and the Professional Business Women of California. Her humorous, motivational, and results-oriented take on leadership, courage, and customer service makes her one of the most effective strategic consultants and speakers working today.

Cindy welcome to *Extreme Excellence!*

Cindy Solomon (Solomon)

Thank you very much David.

Wright

I notice on your card your title is Customer Service Provocateur, what exactly does that mean?

Solomon

I took on the title of provocateur because that philosophy is very different from that of most of my colleagues. Most of the folks in my business, particularly in the customer service world, talk a great deal about training with lists of rules or sets of guidelines in order to create exceptional service. I believe what we really should be doing in our organizations is exactly the opposite of rote memorization of do's and don'ts. True customer service excellence begins with everyone in an organization fully understanding their role and how to make the best possible decisions, not just for the company, but for the customer and for themselves as well.

Wright

I know you began your career in corporate America and left to create a successful consulting practice focused on leadership and customer service, so why and how did you decide to do this?

Solomon

After working in various roles within corporate America including positions at the senior leadership level, I decided it was time to really follow my passion. Even fifteen years ago, I could see the decline of service and the lack of value placed on the relationship between a company and its customers. I could see my own organization consistently ignoring the needs of customers and focusing on internal issues rather than seeking and acting on customer input. As customers ourselves, we see the lack of commitment to creating true customer relationships play out in our own frustrations with companies we work with every day.

I had the good fortune to work in one of the first database building companies in the country and it was there that I really began to see the opportunities companies and brands had in building profitable relationships with their customers. I didn't see anyone out there helping organizations recognize the true value of creating exceptional service and how by doing so, they could directly and positively affect their bottom-line results. I wanted to help organizations to cost effectively, pro-actively, and quickly take action in order to build true customer and employee loyalty. I guess you could say that I decided to become the consultant that I wished I could have hired back in my days in corporate America.

Wright

One of the focuses of your practice is the need for companies to go beyond satisfaction and build a true relationship with their customers. What exactly does this mean and why do you think it's so important?

Solomon

We have seen a transformation over the last five to ten years with regard to how and why customers buy from us. Changes in technology, the media, and the new global marketplace have all had a profound affect on customer behavior. Today, the real issue for most companies is not only how to find the right customers and serve them, but it is just as important to learn what will keep that same customer coming back time after time. We used to think that satisfaction was enough and that if we "on average" kept most of our customers satisfied they would continue to return and reward us with their loyalty.

Unfortunately what we see today is that satisfaction is no longer enough to create true loyalty. As a matter of fact, as Fredrick Reichheld found out in his loyalty research, almost 80 percent of customers who defect from your product or service to a similar product or service note that they are actually satisfied. Said another way, satisfaction simply isn't enough to keep customers coming back to us. We have to find new ways as organizations or brands, as products or services, to build a deeper relationship that creates a true and lasting partnership.

That's why my strategic consulting and speaking practice is focused on how we can energize and motivate entire organizations to create stronger and deeper relationships with our customers. It's the only way to be assured of building true loyalty.

Wright

It seems as though this would be an easy thing for most organizations to accomplish, and yet from my personal experience I know many companies struggle with this. Why do you think that is?

Solomon

I think most organizations approach this idea of creating exceptional service from an orientation of rules and list-making. They believe that if we tell our organization to do these five things, we'll build relationships with our customers. Or, if we do these ten things we'll build good service and keep our customers. It simply doesn't work that way. It is precisely this kind of thinking that defeats most organizations in their quest to build exceptional service and loyalty. It always makes me laugh when I walk into a company and see a big poster on the wall saying, "We put our customers first!" You can bet that if you have to have a poster about it, you're not really doing it.

Another issue for most organizations is that they focus their training efforts primarily on frontline staff. Most organizations assume their leadership is focused on providing exceptional service and that the problem lies with the staff. My experience is that great leadership creates great service and great results. If your organization concentrates its efforts on creating exceptional leaders, they will in turn build teams that excel at service. If organizations focus on creating leaders who coach and support their people, allow their staff to truly think on their feet, provide them with the tools, resources, and most importantly, the skills to do the right thing for customers, great service will always follow.

Focusing your efforts on both developing great leaders and creating well-informed and well-trained staff enables you to start moving the needle from satisfaction to true long-term customer loyalty. It's really about energizing your entire company to think differently about service, not just the front line. This kind of transformation takes a true commitment from the CEO suite throughout the entire organization.

Wright

You talk about great service being created by great leaders and yet they aren't the ones usually on the front lines creating the customer interaction, so why is leadership so important?

Solomon

Great leaders help an organization focus on the right priorities, and generate enthusiasm around that goal. If you have ever worked within any organization, you know that employees reflect their leaders, whether in a positive or negative way. Until we can align our leaders and provide them with the direction and enthusiasm to effectively do their jobs, the rest of the organization cannot align to our purpose. It is through our commitment to building our leaders' skills and abilities that will in turn allow the entire organization to grow and focus on customers.

Leaders must have the communication, coaching, performance management, and motivational skills to be able to engage and inspire their entire organization. For example: If you're an organization of a thousand people, more than likely you have approximately seventy to one hundred and fifty leaders who need to be marching in lockstep to create and grow each of their individual teams. Once you have that type of consistency within a leadership team, great service simply flows from everyone in that team. You have happy, engaged, inspired, and productive employees, and that's what will enable you to finally create true customer loyalty.

Wright

Will you tell me more about your thoughts on leadership and how leaders can be most effective at creating customer focused cultures?

Solomon

It's a question we have all asked ourselves at one point or another. What really differentiates a "great leader" from one who doesn't really measure up? There is a great deal of argument about this topic in academic circles, business circles, and some would even say on the world stage with opinions varying greatly. In my thirty years of experience working for leaders and with leaders, I have found that the formula isn't really all that difficult nor is it something that can't be learned by anyone willing to put in the time and effort to continuously improve their leadership skills.

In my interviews with literally thousands of people regarding leadership, all the anecdotes and stories boil down to four simple elements or steps. Great leaders engage, inspire, enable, and reward. Although these are only four little words, in reality their execution and the ability to truly pursue them are the difference between good and great.

True engagement is based on a leader's ability to communicate the vision of a customer-focused culture and emotionally connect the individuals on his or her team to that vision. It sounds easy but in reality, it is one of the most difficult things leaders must do. It requires them to be completely clear about not only their organizations' goals but more importantly, how their teams can help achieve those goals.

For example, your organization's goals might be to "increase customer loyalty." Well, that seems like a valid goal, but what specifically does your team have to do in order to help the overall organization achieve this goal? This is where a great leader translates the overall vision of the organization into applicable, actionable, and behavioral goals for their own team. If my organization's goal is to "increase customer loyalty," my team's goal might translate into "reduce wait-time on the phones" or "return customer calls within twenty-four hours" or some other behavior commitment that is easy to execute and measure. Once members of a team fully understand how their behaviors directly link to the organization's goals, you have true "Engagement."

The next element is to create real inspiration around the goal of building true customer partnerships and loyalty. Most of us think of inspiration as the "We have a dream" type of inspiration where in reality, inspiration can come in many, different forms. Great leaders inspire by ensuring that each team member feels they have a meaningful role in achieving the goals of the organization. They should feel they are working within a team where their talents and skills are recognized and appreciated.

If you look back on when you have felt most inspired, my bet is that it was when you were working toward a goal that you were emotionally attached to and in which you felt you played a meaningful and important role. Inspiration relates back to allowing people to feel their behaviors and efforts have a direct affect on the achievement of a goal. Constant communication and discussion surrounding your goals and achievements are vital to inspiring your team even when the going gets tough.

I know the word "enable" has gotten a bad rap over the past few years, but we need to again think of it in the context of how it helps us achieve our goal of creating a customer-focused culture. In the dictionary, "enable is defined as "to make able, make ready, equip." So much of our leadership activities today are wasted on "managing tasks" rather than "leading and enabling people." Clearly, every leader needs to manage some administrative and corporate activities, but many leaders don't place enough emphasis on developing, coaching, training, and enabling their teams. This is the most important and usually the most overlooked element of a leader's work each day. Great leaders spend over 80 percent of their time coaching, training, and developing the individuals on their teams.

How many of us could say that is how we are spending our time *or* how many of us could say we get this type of attention from our leaders? When faced with this information, most leaders will automatically say, "I don't have enough time to coach/train/develop my people." If that is the case, then why do they need a leader?

Performance management isn't as hard as the name implies; it is simply taking a few moments each day to talk with your team members about their skills and how they can be continuously improving them in order to achieve your goals. Many of us have come to assume performance management is a once-a-year review, and that should be enough to build performance. This would be similar to trying to learn to play golf or to ski with only one lesson. Great performance management conversations can take as little as two minutes and can have an enormous affect on your team's ability to succeed. These types of activities all help you enable your team members to learn, grow, to be challenged, and to succeed. Now *that's* great leadership.

The last step in the process is often the most overlooked. The moment I begin talking about "reward," most people assume I mean financial rewards. The statistics are overwhelming in this area and they aren't what you think they might be. In most surveys conducted around the question, "How do you keep your most important employees happy and productive?" the results are clear—money is usually fourth on a list of the five most important elements. Most often, within that top four is a list of "rewards" that don't cost an organization a penny, such as positive recognition, training, a clear idea of career path, feeling cared about, flexibility in the work environment, additional responsibilities and challenges, feeling a part of decision-making, a feeling of having a meaningful role. I think all of us would agree that the dollars must be within reason, but I think we would also agree that these other elements of "reward" are much more important when it comes to staying engaged and excited in a workplace.

Wright

I have one last question. Personally, throughout the last thirty or forty years, I have attended more seminars, listened to more tapes and CDs, and read more books on customer service than any other single topic, and I think most of my friends who own businesses tell me the same thing—it seems that customer service is the lowest it has ever been in the history of most companies today. Why is that true?

Solomon

Unfortunately, you are absolutely right. Customers are changing and our organizations aren't changing with them. There are many factors I share with my clients that deeply affect their ability to provide service, but for today, let me discuss three of the trends I believe are most important.

The first trend it that time is the new currency. Customers today are requiring everyone they deal with to do things faster, more easily and, ideally, more effectively. The most interesting phenomenon is that many of us (myself included) are willing to pay a little more if in fact that premium will allow us to interact more quickly with a company. Examples of "premium service for a charge" abound for the simple reason that we all feel we have limited time for a multitude of actions. I think this is a win-win for all of us if we can concentrate our efforts on creating efficient processes, easy interaction with customers, and pro-active and knowledgeable employees who can reduce the time needed to deal with us. This is particularly an issue for companies that have been successful in the past. The arrogance of success is to think that what you did yesterday is good enough for tomorrow. I think all of our own experiences show us that this is simply not true today.

Due to this focus on time, our expectations as customers have increased a great deal. We are much more demanding, more educated, and have more choices than ever before. It is this phenomenon of exponentially increasing expectations that has changed the dynamic of who really is our competitor. In the good old days, if I sold widgets, the company down the street that also sold widgets was my competition. Today, our competition is any company who has sold a product or service to our customer where that customer was not only pleased but thrilled with the service that was provided. I think you would agree that once we receive great service or use an easy transaction to buy a product or even save time, we begin to wish all of our interactions were that easy.

In my case, I wish every company that I interacted with as a customer was as easy to deal with as my favorite local takeout restaurant. Every time I call them to place an order, they already know my name, my address, my usual order, and even my credit card information. I am off the phone in a matter of seconds, which is not only efficient, but as importantly, makes me feel as if they know and care about me. I wish my interactions with my credit card company or my local dry cleaners could be as easy and fun! That's how we all need to begin thinking about competition. It can come from anywhere. The good news is that we can utilize our own personal experiences in any industry to help our own organizations improve.

The third trend driving customer behavior is that without a relationship, there are no second chances. Organizations that understand this begin to understand the importance of every single contact with a customer. A way to think about this is to keep it simple. Think about your favorite restaurant. One night you visit and for whatever reason your experience is not up to its usual standard. Possibly the food is a little off, or your server isn't as responsive or as nice as usual. If you are like most people, you walk out of the restaurant, shake your head, and think, "How odd." Again, if you are like most people, you will go back again and give them another chance. Now, what if that was your first visit to this particular restaurant? Would you ever go back? Not only do most people not go back, but they also tell their friends and neighbors that the restaurant is terrible. That's what I mean by saying that without a relationship, there are no second chances.

The organizations I believe that will succeed in the future will be constantly seeking new ways to gain ground against these three customer trends.

Wright

I've heard from many of your clients that you consistently leave your audiences on their feet and ready to make positive changes, so will you tell our readers your secret in creating this reaction?

Solomon

It first begins with passion for my topic and passion for helping organizations create exceptional leaders and cultures. Also, because I have worked in corporate America and have shared many of the experiences of my audiences, I can empathize and approach my topic realistically. There is nothing more annoying than having a consultant come in and tell you how to think or what to do and then find out the person has never been on your side of the table.

I also approach each organization, each team or, for that matter, each day as a new experience—a new way for me to learn as much from my clients as my clients do from me. I begin each speech with a quote: "In the mind of a beginner all things are possible; in the mind of an expert only a few . . ." and I believe it is this perspective that allows us to believe we can do anything. It allows us to create new and positive change. As an example, I didn't set out to become a nationally recognized speaker. I originally set out to try and help companies do the right thing for their customers and their employees. I discovered that if I went through a series of interviews—particularly with frontline staff—prior to presenting any speech, it enabled me to fully understand the organization, what its challenges are, and customize a presentation that resonates and enables change and learning.

As I've continued to grow and my practice has grown, I've kept that philosophy of truly getting to know each particular client before I speak to him or her, or certainly consult for the person. That process enables me to be heard as an insider and to be in a position to poke a bit of fun at the organization. That seems to endear me to many people in organizations and it also shows my respect for them and their challenges.

Having similar experiences, both in corporate America and as a successful entrepreneur, is also very important. As I mentioned earlier, I know what it's like to deal with a boss and a budget and ever-changing priorities in a volatile market place. I understand what those situations feel like because in my corporate career, rising through the ranks, I felt and dealt with those pressures. That enables me to provide more real-life, realistic, and attainable goals and tools for organizations to utilize quickly and effectively.

Probably my greatest asset is that I'm a bit of a frustrated stand-up comic, and have a great deal humor about myself and about the world around me. The ability to laugh at our challenges while addressing them in a realistic way enables my message to be heard and absorbed. I think humor certainly opens us up to doing things differently. It also makes some difficult things a little less painful and that's what helps people more effectively do the right thing.

Wright

I know you only take a few consulting clients each year, so how do you decide which clients you will work with?

Solomon

That's always a tough decision for me because speaking as much as I do doesn't leave a lot of time for the deep-dive, in-depth, consulting work that I so enjoy. Limiting my larger consulting clients to a few a year enables me to give each of them more of my time, my energy, and my focus. I tend to identify clients who meet what I believe are the three steps to success when it comes to creating customer-focused cultures.

First, you need a committed senior leadership team. I have found that leaders in many companies know they need to be customer-focused but lack the courage and commitment at the higher levels of the organization to truly make the change. Of course, if they call you and want to send you a big check, it must seem as though they are committed. It isn't necessarily so. You can hear a lot of talk in organizations about wanting to build true leaders, and yet enabling accountability or giving positive reinforcement, coaching, or mentoring does not always happen.

I tend to ask CEOs one question: how much time do you spend working with frontline staff and interacting directly with your customers? If it's less than say a day a week or if they're only dealing with the largest clients, then they're never really seeing what frontline staff or frontline customers are going through. That already shows me that there may not be a level of commitment at the senior level.

Second, I look at how willing the client is to do things differently. I go back to the quote I mentioned earlier—in the mind of a beginner all things are possible. How willing is the client to be a beginner again? How willing is the organization to risk potential short-term failure with new ideas and new ways of doing things that will lead to future success? I'm a firm believer that every failure is simply another step toward success.

The third question I ask is how energized is the leadership team as a whole to build their skills and become better at what they are doing? I work with organizations that may be new and have an average five-year tenure for employee or leader. I also work with organizations that have average tenure in the thirty-year range. Regardless of tenure, almost every leader and every frontline employee is passionate about what they're doing and certainly passionate about their customers. It's up to me to be able to assess their willingness to try to do things a little differently. It's like learning any new skill or even sport. It might be uncomfortable for the short term, but in order to get to our end goal of creating a truly customer-focused culture, we have to risk it together.

If potential clients can successfully navigate those three questions, I am thrilled to work with them to create an even more successful and loyalty focused organization.

Wright

Well, what a great conversation. I really do appreciate all this time you've taken with me this morning to answer these questions. I learned a lot and I am positive that our readers will.

Solomon

Thank you so much David, it's been my pleasure.

Wright

Today we've been talking with Cindy Solomon. Cindy is founder and CEO of Solomon and Associates, an organization committed to helping organizations build long-term as well as profitable relationships with customers, leaders, and employees. As we have found today, her humorous, motivational, and results-oriented take on leadership and customer service has made her one of the most effective strategic consultants and speakers working today.

Cindy, thank you so much for being with us on *Extreme Excellence*.

Solomon

Thank you, David.

About the Author

As one of the most sought after consultants and keynote speakers in the country today Cindy brings her provocative and innovative insights to literally thousands of leaders and hundreds of organizations each year. Cindy's client list includes a who's who of national and international corporations, associations and some of the largest gatherings of leaders in the country including; Microsoft, Eli Lilly & Company, Genentech, Oracle, National Nurse Practitioners Association, Professional Business Women of California, Telluride Ski & Golf Company, Cisco, Pfizer and Syracuse University to name only a few. Cindy's humorous, motivational, and results-oriented take on leadership and customer service makes her one of the most effective strategic consultants, workshop leaders, and speakers working today.

Cindy Solomon
Solomon & Associates, Inc.
San Francisco & Denver Offices
Phone: 415-401-8646
www.CindySolomon.com
Cindy@CindySolomon.com